ARMY OF GOD

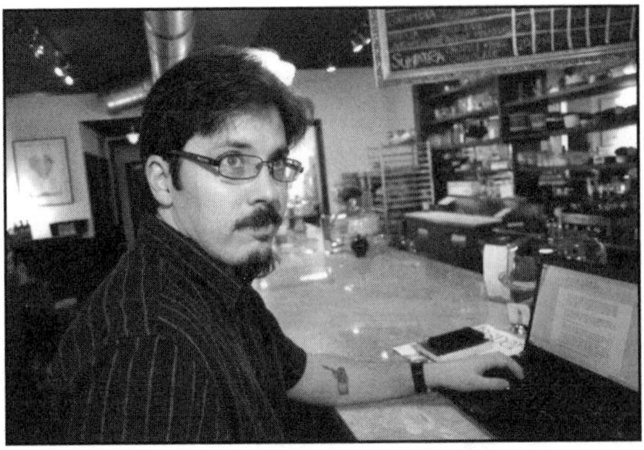

Photo by Thomas Hammond

DAVID AXE is a freelance reporter based in Columbia, South Carolina. Since 2005 he has reported from Iraq, Afghanistan, Lebanon, Somalia, Chad, Congo, and other conflict zones for *Wired*, the BBC, *Salon*, *Esquire*, C-SPAN, Voice of America, and many others. David is the author of several graphic novels, including *War Fix, War is Boring*, and most recently, *The Accidental Candidate: The Rise and Fall of Alvin Greene*. David blogs at www.warisboring.com.

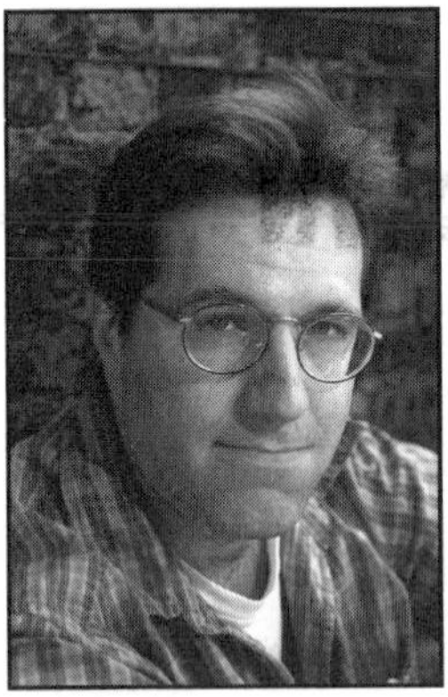

Photo by Seth Kushner

TIM HAMILTON is a Brooklyn artist who has produced illustrations for the *New York Times*, *Cicada Magazine*, DC comics, Marvel comics, *Mad* magazine, *Nickelodeon* magazine, and Lifetime. He adapted Ray Bradbury's *Fahrenheit 451* into a graphic novel, which was nominated for an Eisner award.

ARMY OF GOD

Joseph Kony's War in Central Africa

DAVID AXE *and* TIM HAMILTON

PUBLICAFFAIRS
New York

Published in the United States by PublicAffairs™, a Member of the Perseus Books Group

PublicAffairs books are available at special discounts for bulk purchases in the U.S. by corporations, institutions, and other organizations. For more information, please contact the Special Markets Department at the Perseus Books Group, 2300 Chestnut Street, Suite 200, Philadelphia, PA 19103, call (800) 810-4145, ext. 5000, or e-mail special.markets@perseusbooks.com.

Book Design by David Axe and Tim Hamilton

Library of Congress Control Number: 2012955375
ISBN 978-1-61039-299-0 (PB orig.)
ISBN 978-1-61039-300-3 (EB)

First Edition
10 9 8 7 6 5 4 3 2 1

To Windsor Cowart. Thanks for putting up with me. — *David Axe*

TABLE OF CONTENTS

PREFACE

I WAS NO STRANGER to war. But to me this war was, well, strange.

The fighting in the Democratic Republic of Congo was like nothing I'd experienced in my then five years as a war correspondent for *Wired*, Voice of America, and other media outlets. I'd covered conflicts in Iraq, Afghanistan, Lebanon, East Timor, Somalia, Chad, and other countries. I'd witnessed gunfights, bombings, suicide attacks, artillery duels, airstrikes, and mob violence. I'd been shot at, blown up, arrested, and kidnapped *twice*.

But I'd never before seen the kind of cruelty that's routine in Congo's overlapping rebellions, terror campaigns, and abusive internal security deployments. Bullets are expensive; machetes are a favored weapon. But even machetes are expensive compared to one implement that's totally free: the human body. In a world where rape as a weapon of war is increasingly rare, in Congo sexual violence is still a preferred tactic. It's with good reason that one U.N. official dubbed the DRC the "rape capital of the world."

There is no single war in Congo, there are several. As I write these words the DRC is a battleground for a rebellion of former army soldiers calling themselves the March 23 (M23) movement—and for the remnants of the Rwandan Hutu Power group, known by its French acronym, FDLR. The country has become a theater for tense, and sometimes deadly, face-offs between Congolese government troops and those of neighboring Rwanda, an historic foe of the DRC.

But most prominently to the outside world, Congo is the base of the Lord's Resistance Army, a once-Ugandan rebel group that fled its homeland and, loosed from its original political aims, now fights to survive. Dominated by its mysterious, volatile founder Joseph Kony and governed by a complex body of rules, customs, and superstitions, the LRA is ostensibly a fundamentalist Christian religious movement, an army of God. In reality it bears no resemblance to Christian institutions elsewhere. Its methods are rape and pillage. Its major aim is to sustain itself.

It is neither the first nor the most destructive armed group to ever occupy the DRC; it won't be the last group to terrorize the Congolese forest. But the LRA is unique for its odd, even terrifying, culture—and for its tenacity. Constantly on the move and periodically refreshed with the enslaved and gradually brainwashed young men and women it captures on the march, the LRA has survived in Congo for nearly a decade despite the efforts of several governments and world bodies to destroy it. Kony's fighters—who currently number between 100 and 600, according to the most reliable sources—have killed thousands, abducted tens of thousands, and displaced hundreds of thousands.

It was 2010 when I decided to go to Congo. My reasons were deeply personal: By then I had reported from all the worst places I could think of except Congo. Like Iraq, Afghanistan, and Somalia, it was on a secret list inscribed on my heart in black ink. I went because I could no longer make excuses to myself for not going. I went seeking answers:

Where had the LRA come from? I'd researched the formal answer: it came from northern Uganda during a time of civil unrest. But my research didn't answer the more fundamental question. What ambitions, convictions, fears, and impulses motivated Kony and his followers? I wanted to map the emotional and spiritual landscape of the group.

Likewise, what was it like living under the shadow of the LRA? Was it hard to survive in the remotest part of a remote country where the government is often as frightening as the rebels, terrorists, and criminals? What did it feel like knowing the killers could strike at any time—and that likely no one would come to your aid when they did? What about the children who've never known a world without the LRA? Kids are adaptable, but what did it mean to adapt to a world of rape and bloodshed?

I also wanted to gauge the rest of the world's responsibility. What, if anything, could and should the world do about the LRA? Without a doubt, Congo's long history as the subject of uncaring colonial powers had contributed to its present lawlessness. Already the DRC was the subject of one of the largest U.N. peacekeeping operations ever. Was more foreign intervention the solution or the problem? As a member of the Western media, was there anything I could do to help?

My timing was fortuitous. In late 2010, Congo was at a crossroads. Years of Chinese investment had transformed the infrastructure of the capital, Kinshasa. Growing ties with the outside world meant more trade, incrementally better governance, and greater demand among everyday people for goods, services, rights, and real democracy. After several botched military operations against the LRA, the U.N. was rethinking its approach to peacekeeping.

And the U.S. government, all but absent from the DRC for many years, was getting more involved. American aid workers and advocates were on the ground. Secretary of State Hillary Clinton visited Congo in late 2009. In May 2010, President Barack Obama signed a law requiring his administration to formulate an official strategy for defeating the LRA. Initial contingents of American troops were arriving to hand out medicine and help train the *Forces Armees de la Republique Democratique du Congo* (FARDC), the Congolese army. In a very real way my own presence represented another small facet of the increasing U.S. involvement in the DRC.

I flew into Kinshasa in September 2010. In that teeming city of eight million in the DRC's more-developed west, I met up with members of the North Dakota Army National Guard, deployed to Congo for a medical exercise with the FARDC. Their goal: to teach the Congolese army how to actually help their own people.

After the American soldiers departed, I shifted gears. I spoke to the U.S. embassy about efforts to reform the Congolese government. I interviewed the heads of aid groups struggling to shore up the collapse of eastern communities under siege by the LRA and other armed groups. I visited a home for former child soldiers who had been liberated from the groups enslaving them.

Then I flew east in a plane belonging to the U.N. World Food Program. I landed in Dungu, a small town deep in the heart of LRA country. The FARDC camped on the outskirts near two bases controlled by the U.N. peacekeeping force. Aid groups maintained offices in town. The Catholic Church, headed by native and white priests, served as the glue that held all the disparate efforts together. I attended a church service one morning to see for myself the depth and power of Congolese faith.

I visited the troops and the humanitarians. I accompanied military patrols escorting food aid to nearby settlements. I observed the heartbreaking daily rounds of a young priest who served as a sort of walking hotline for myriad pleas by the sick, injured, and destitute. And I met the victims—men, women, boys, and girls who had been assaulted, kidnapped, enslaved, raped, and mutilated by the LRA.

My interview with a sweet, shy, 13-year-old girl I call Patricia was the critical moment for me, the instant I came to truly understand the human cost of the LRA's two decades of pillage—and the instant I decided to write this graphic novel.

In 2009 Patricia, her brother, and father fled an LRA attack on the town of Duru. The rebel fighters intercepted the three in the forest. They killed the father and took Patricia and her brother back to their camp. The LRA forced the brother to work. Patricia was "married" to a rebel in a mock ceremony. Then he raped her.

As if that weren't enough, the rebels handed Patricia a machete and ordered her to kill a villager. If she refused, they would beat her. She didn't say so explicitly, but I sensed that Patricia understood what would happen if she did as she was told. She would become not just a captive of the LRA. She would become *one of them*.

She refused to kill ... and suffered the consequences. Later, liberated by Ugandan troops, she and her brother were brought to Dungu for rehabilitation. Patricia was obviously deeply traumatized. But in rejecting violence she kept her soul. And in that holy act of defiance, she became a warrior in the true army of God.

David Axe
COLUMBIA, S.C.
NOVEMBER 2012

PROLOGUE: THE CONGO

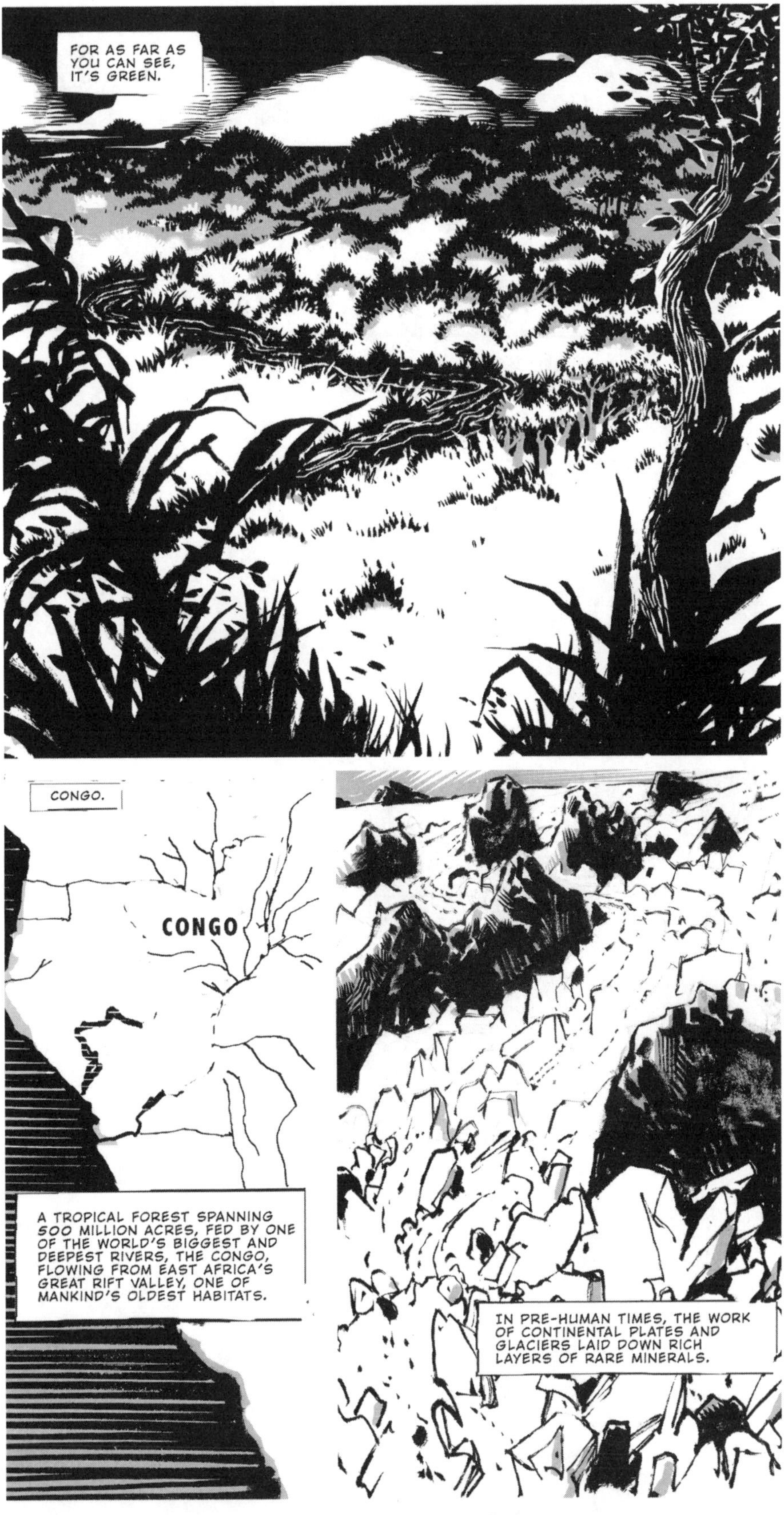
FOR AS FAR AS YOU CAN SEE, IT'S GREEN.
CONGO.
CONGO
A TROPICAL FOREST SPANNING 500 MILLION ACRES, FED BY ONE OF THE WORLD'S BIGGEST AND DEEPEST RIVERS, THE CONGO, FLOWING FROM EAST AFRICA'S GREAT RIFT VALLEY, ONE OF MANKIND'S OLDEST HABITATS.
IN PRE-HUMAN TIMES, THE WORK OF CONTINENTAL PLATES AND GLACIERS LAID DOWN RICH LAYERS OF RARE MINERALS.

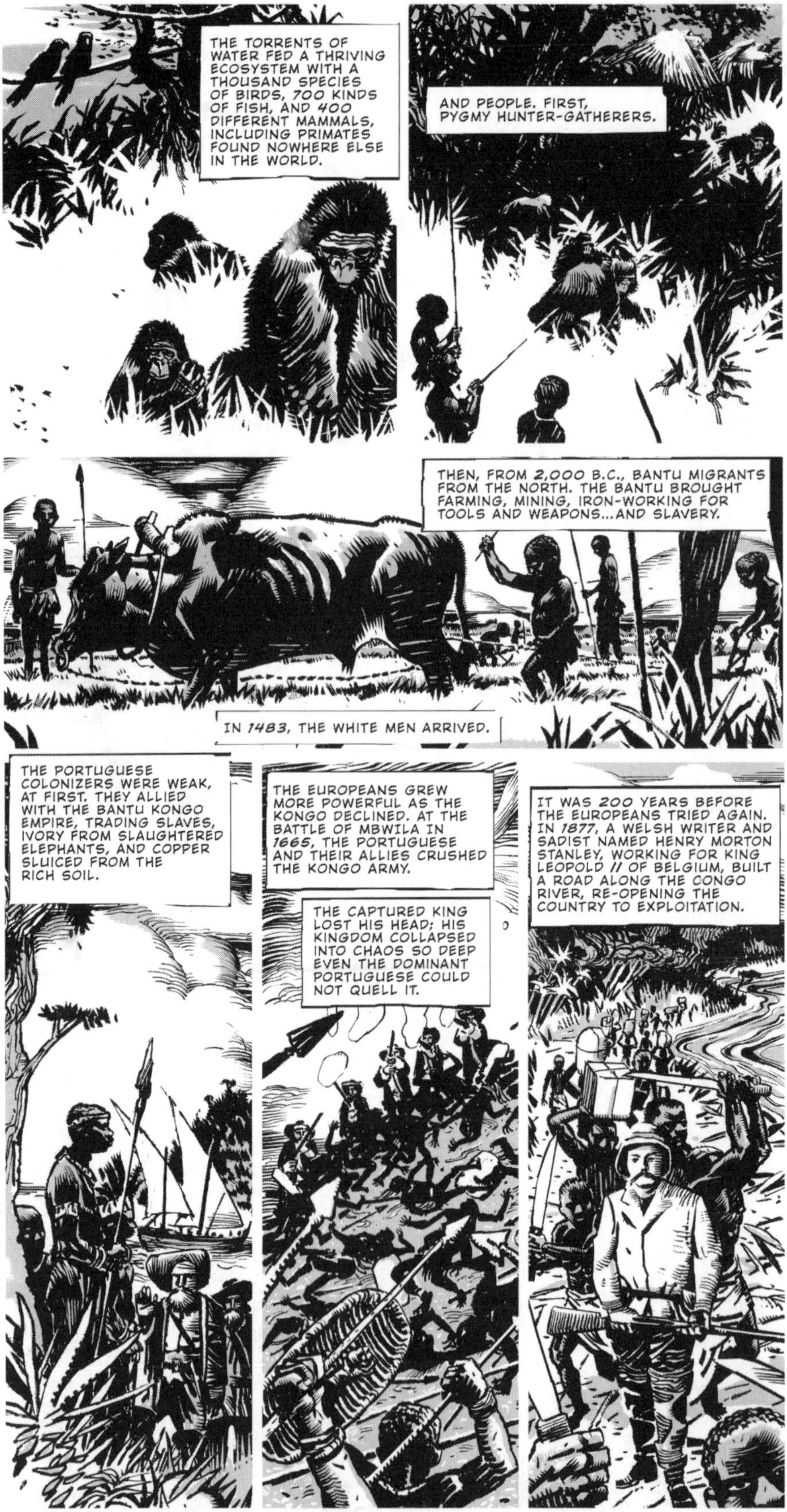
THE TORRENTS OF WATER FED A THRIVING ECOSYSTEM WITH A THOUSAND SPECIES OF BIRDS, 700 KINDS OF FISH, AND 400 DIFFERENT MAMMALS, INCLUDING PRIMATES FOUND NOWHERE ELSE IN THE WORLD.
AND PEOPLE. FIRST, PYGMY HUNTER-GATHERERS.
THEN, FROM 2,000 B.C., BANTU MIGRANTS FROM THE NORTH. THE BANTU BROUGHT FARMING, MINING, IRON-WORKING FOR TOOLS AND WEAPONS...AND SLAVERY.
IN 1483, THE WHITE MEN ARRIVED.
THE PORTUGUESE COLONIZERS WERE WEAK, AT FIRST. THEY ALLIED WITH THE BANTU KONGO EMPIRE, TRADING SLAVES, IVORY FROM SLAUGHTERED ELEPHANTS, AND COPPER SLUICED FROM THE RICH SOIL.
THE EUROPEANS GREW MORE POWERFUL AS THE KONGO DECLINED. AT THE BATTLE OF MBWILA IN 1665, THE PORTUGUESE AND THEIR ALLIES CRUSHED THE KONGO ARMY.
THE CAPTURED KING LOST HIS HEAD; HIS KINGDOM COLLAPSED INTO CHAOS SO DEEP EVEN THE DOMINANT PORTUGUESE COULD NOT QUELL IT.
IT WAS 200 YEARS BEFORE THE EUROPEANS TRIED AGAIN. IN 1877, A WELSH WRITER AND SADIST NAMED HENRY MORTON STANLEY, WORKING FOR KING LEOPOLD II OF BELGIUM, BUILT A ROAD ALONG THE CONGO RIVER, RE-OPENING THE COUNTRY TO EXPLOITATION.

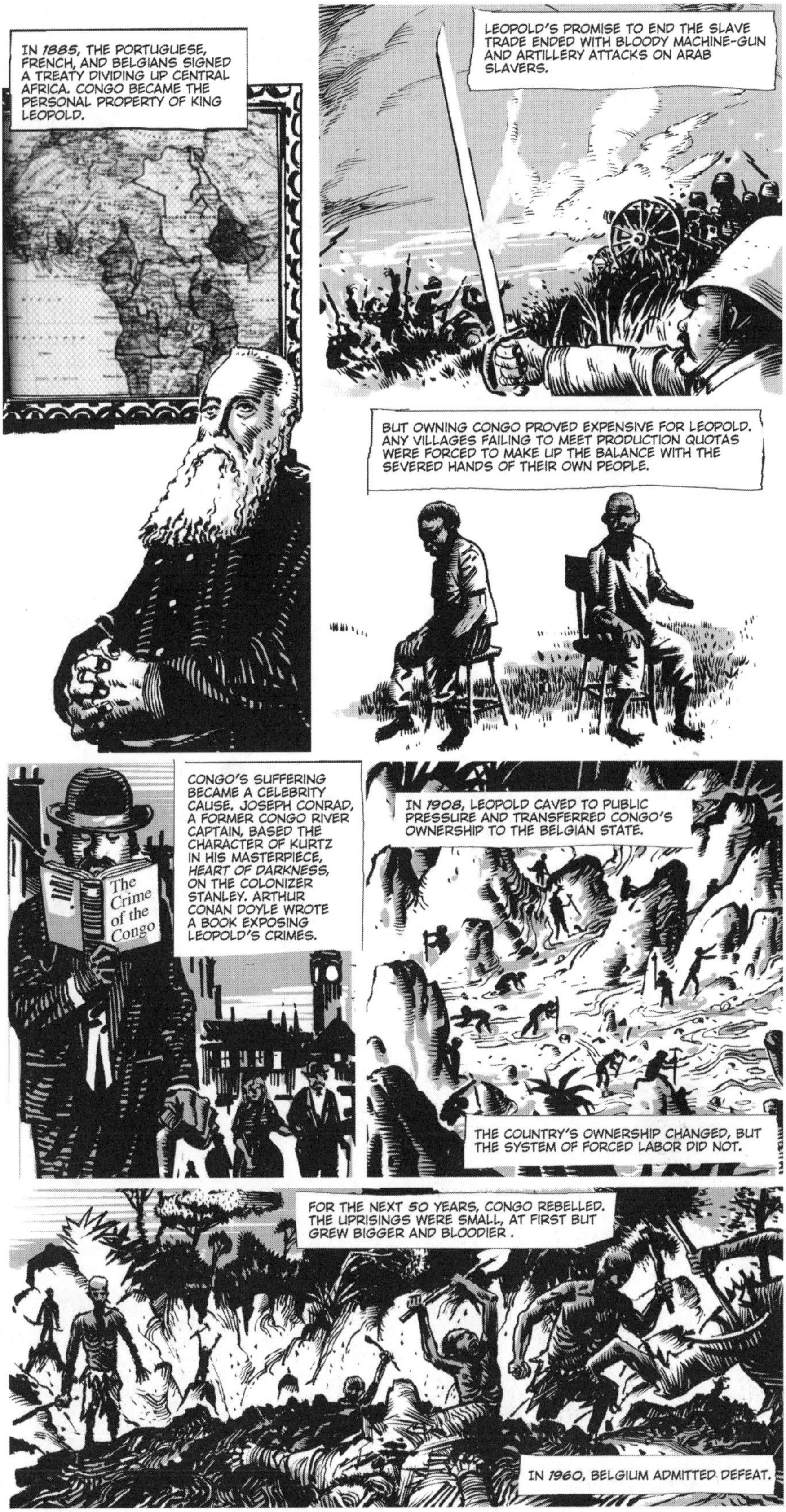
IN 1885, THE PORTUGUESE, FRENCH, AND BELGIANS SIGNED A TREATY DIVIDING UP CENTRAL AFRICA. CONGO BECAME THE PERSONAL PROPERTY OF KING LEOPOLD.
LEOPOLD'S PROMISE TO END THE SLAVE TRADE ENDED WITH BLOODY MACHINE-GUN AND ARTILLERY ATTACKS ON ARAB SLAVERS.
BUT OWNING CONGO PROVED EXPENSIVE FOR LEOPOLD. ANY VILLAGES FAILING TO MEET PRODUCTION QUOTAS WERE FORCED TO MAKE UP THE BALANCE WITH THE SEVERED HANDS OF THEIR OWN PEOPLE.
The Crime of the Congo
CONGO'S SUFFERING BECAME A CELEBRITY CAUSE. JOSEPH CONRAD, A FORMER CONGO RIVER CAPTAIN, BASED THE CHARACTER OF KURTZ IN HIS MASTERPIECE, HEART OF DARKNESS, ON THE COLONIZER STANLEY. ARTHUR CONAN DOYLE WROTE A BOOK EXPOSING LEOPOLD'S CRIMES.
IN 1908, LEOPOLD CAVED TO PUBLIC PRESSURE AND TRANSFERRED CONGO'S OWNERSHIP TO THE BELGIAN STATE.
THE COUNTRY'S OWNERSHIP CHANGED, BUT THE SYSTEM OF FORCED LABOR DID NOT.
FOR THE NEXT 50 YEARS, CONGO REBELLED. THE UPRISINGS WERE SMALL, AT FIRST BUT GREW BIGGER AND BLOODIER .
IN 1960, BELGIUM ADMITTED DEFEAT.

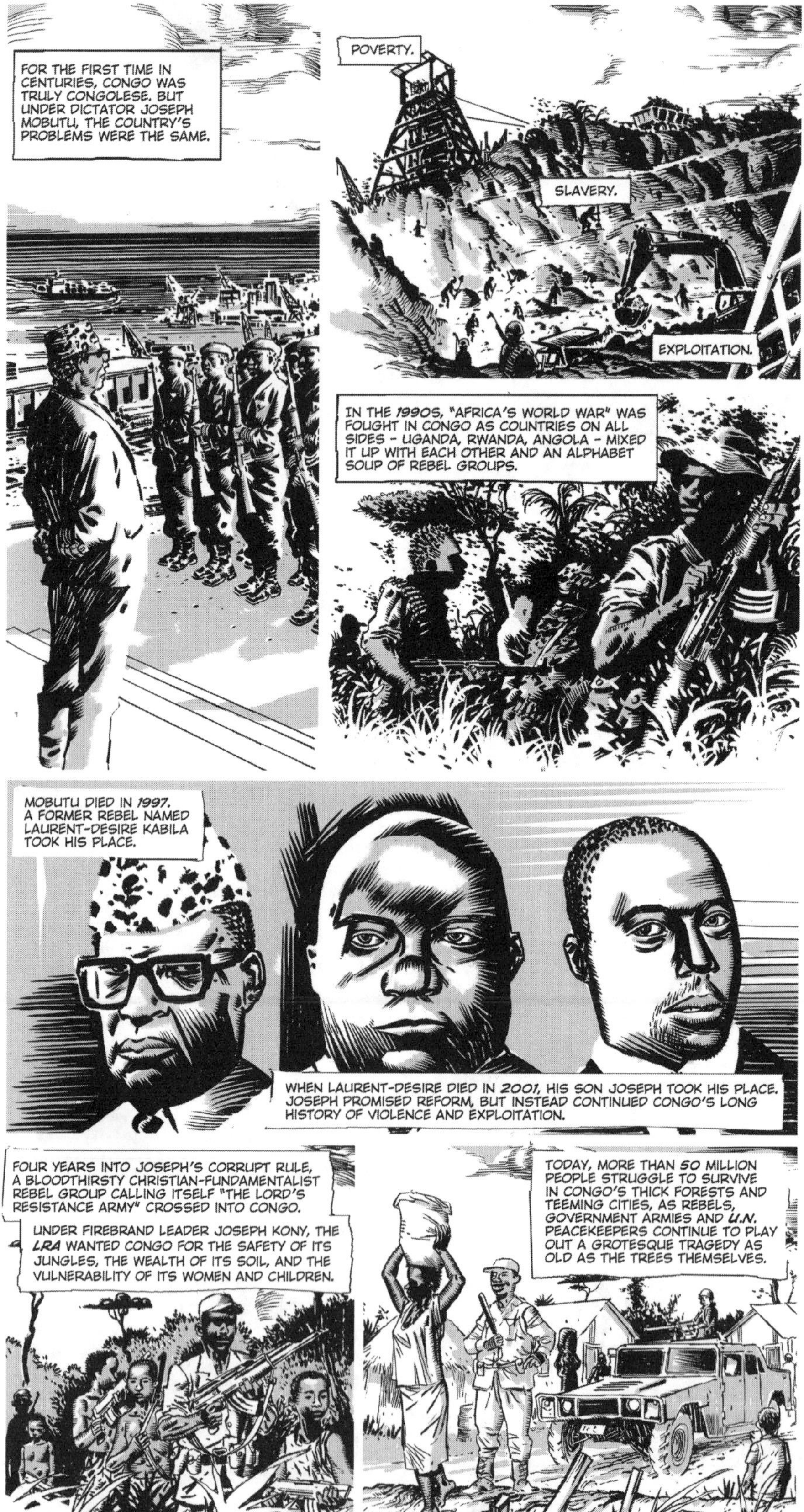
FOR THE FIRST TIME IN CENTURIES, CONGO WAS TRULY CONGOLESE. BUT UNDER DICTATOR JOSEPH MOBUTU, THE COUNTRY'S PROBLEMS WERE THE SAME.
POVERTY.
SLAVERY.
EXPLOITATION.
IN THE 1990S, "AFRICA'S WORLD WAR" WAS FOUGHT IN CONGO AS COUNTRIES ON ALL SIDES – UGANDA, RWANDA, ANGOLA – MIXED IT UP WITH EACH OTHER AND AN ALPHABET SOUP OF REBEL GROUPS.
MOBUTU DIED IN 1997. A FORMER REBEL NAMED LAURENT-DESIRE KABILA TOOK HIS PLACE.
WHEN LAURENT-DESIRE DIED IN 2001, HIS SON JOSEPH TOOK HIS PLACE. JOSEPH PROMISED REFORM, BUT INSTEAD CONTINUED CONGO'S LONG HISTORY OF VIOLENCE AND EXPLOITATION.
FOUR YEARS INTO JOSEPH'S CORRUPT RULE, A BLOODTHIRSTY CHRISTIAN-FUNDAMENTALIST REBEL GROUP CALLING ITSELF "THE LORD'S RESISTANCE ARMY" CROSSED INTO CONGO.
UNDER FIREBRAND LEADER JOSEPH KONY, THE LRA WANTED CONGO FOR THE SAFETY OF ITS JUNGLES, THE WEALTH OF ITS SOIL, AND THE VULNERABILITY OF ITS WOMEN AND CHILDREN.
TODAY, MORE THAN 50 MILLION PEOPLE STRUGGLE TO SURVIVE IN CONGO'S THICK FORESTS AND TEEMING CITIES, AS REBELS, GOVERNMENT ARMIES AND U.N. PEACEKEEPERS CONTINUE TO PLAY OUT A GROTESQUE TRAGEDY AS OLD AS THE TREES THEMSELVES.

CHAPTER ONE: THE TEACHER

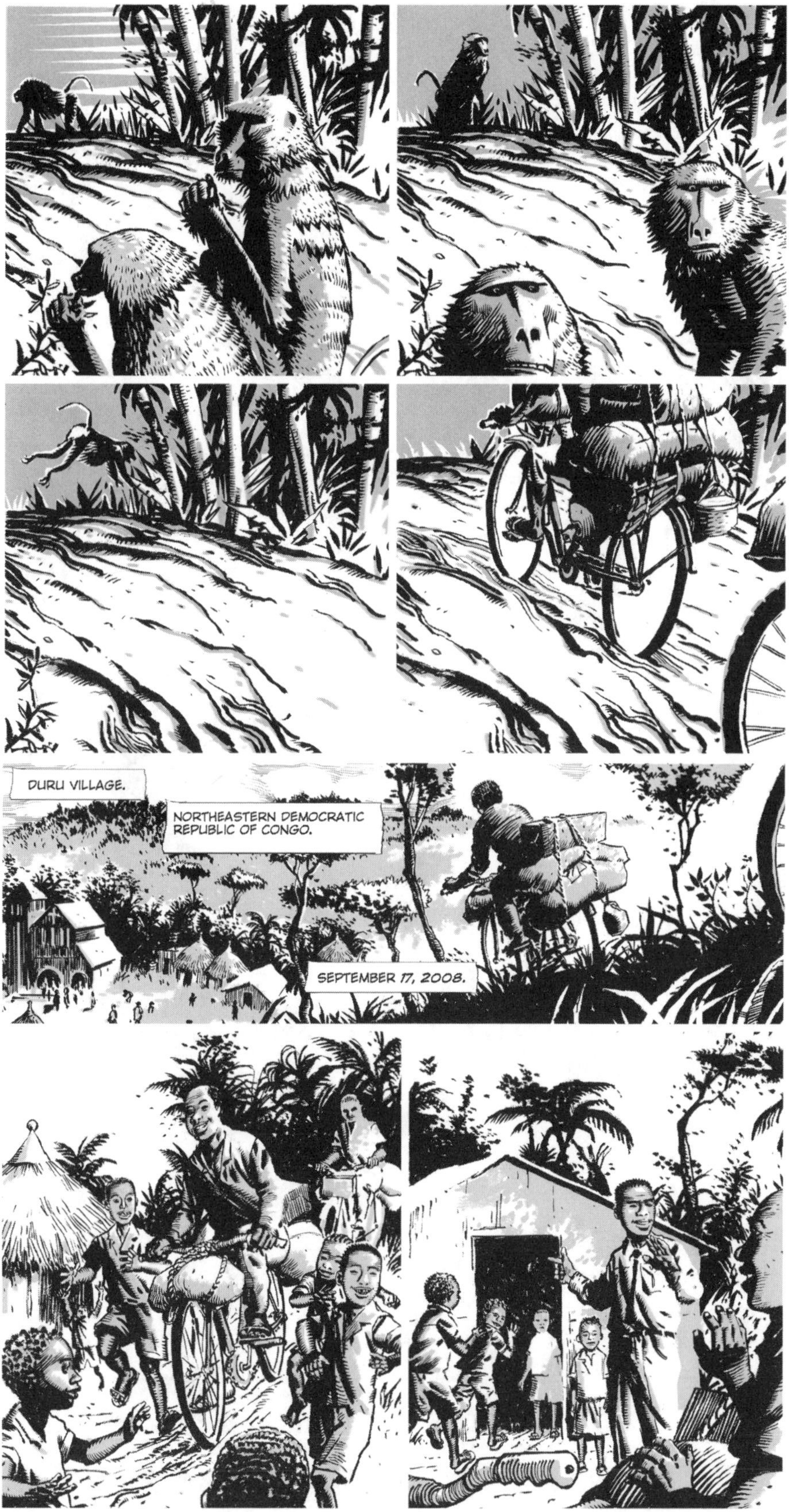
DURU VILLAGE.
NORTHEASTERN DEMOCRATIC REPUBLIC OF CONGO.
SEPTEMBER 17, 2008.

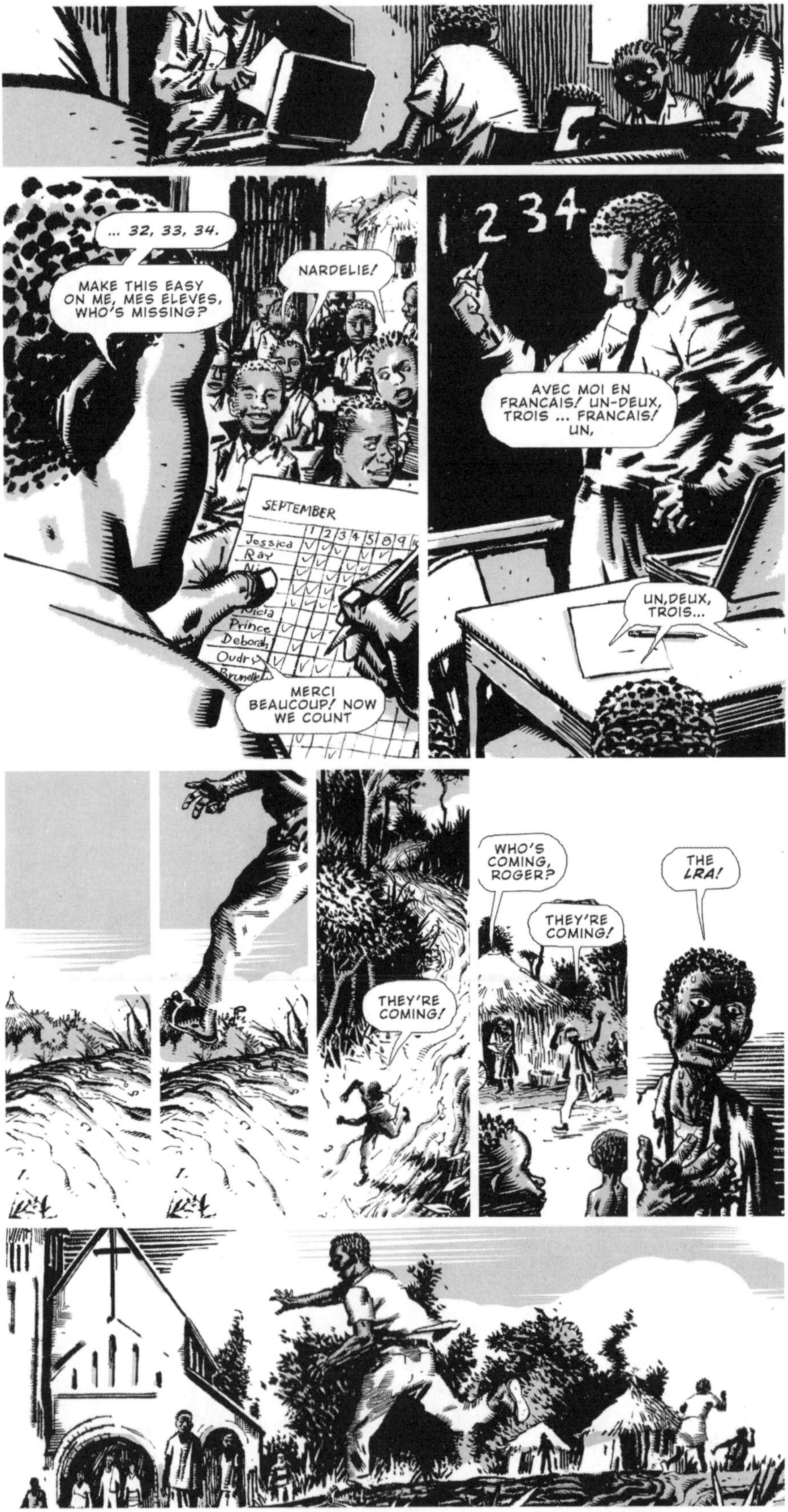
... 32, 33, 34.
MAKE THIS EASY ON ME, MES ELEVES, WHO'S MISSING?
NARDELIE!
SEPTEMBER
Jessica
Ray
Prince
Deborah
Oudry
MERCI BEAUCOUP! NOW WE COUNT
1 2 3 4
AVEC MOI EN FRANCAIS! UN-DEUX, TROIS ... FRANCAIS! UN,
UN,DEUX, TROIS...
THEY'RE COMING!
WHO'S COMING, ROGER?
THEY'RE COMING!
THE LRA!

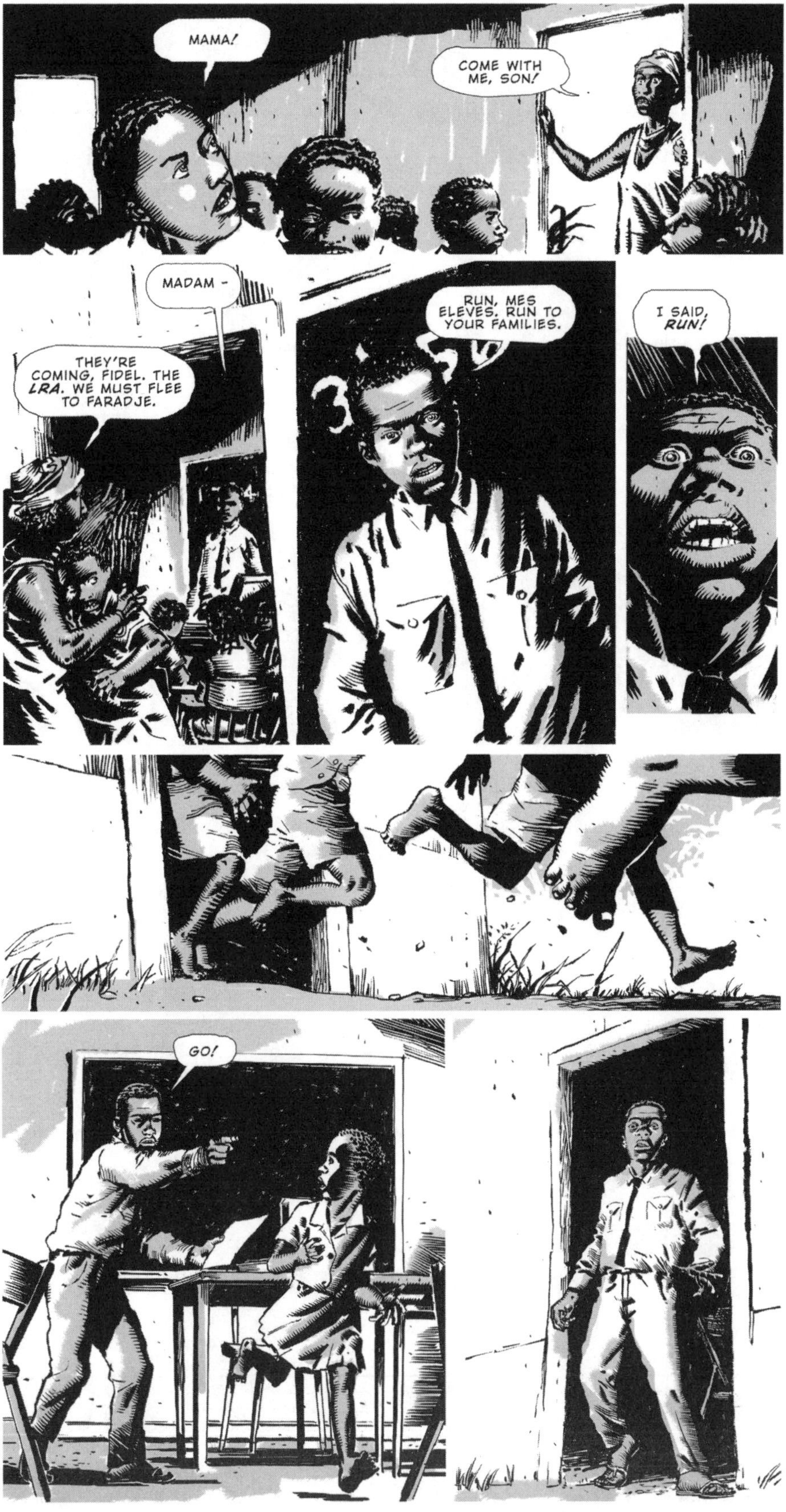
MAMA!
COME WITH ME, SON!
MADAM -
THEY'RE COMING, FIDEL. THE LRA. WE MUST FLEE TO FARADJE.
RUN, MES ELEVES. RUN TO YOUR FAMILIES.
I SAID, RUN!
GO!

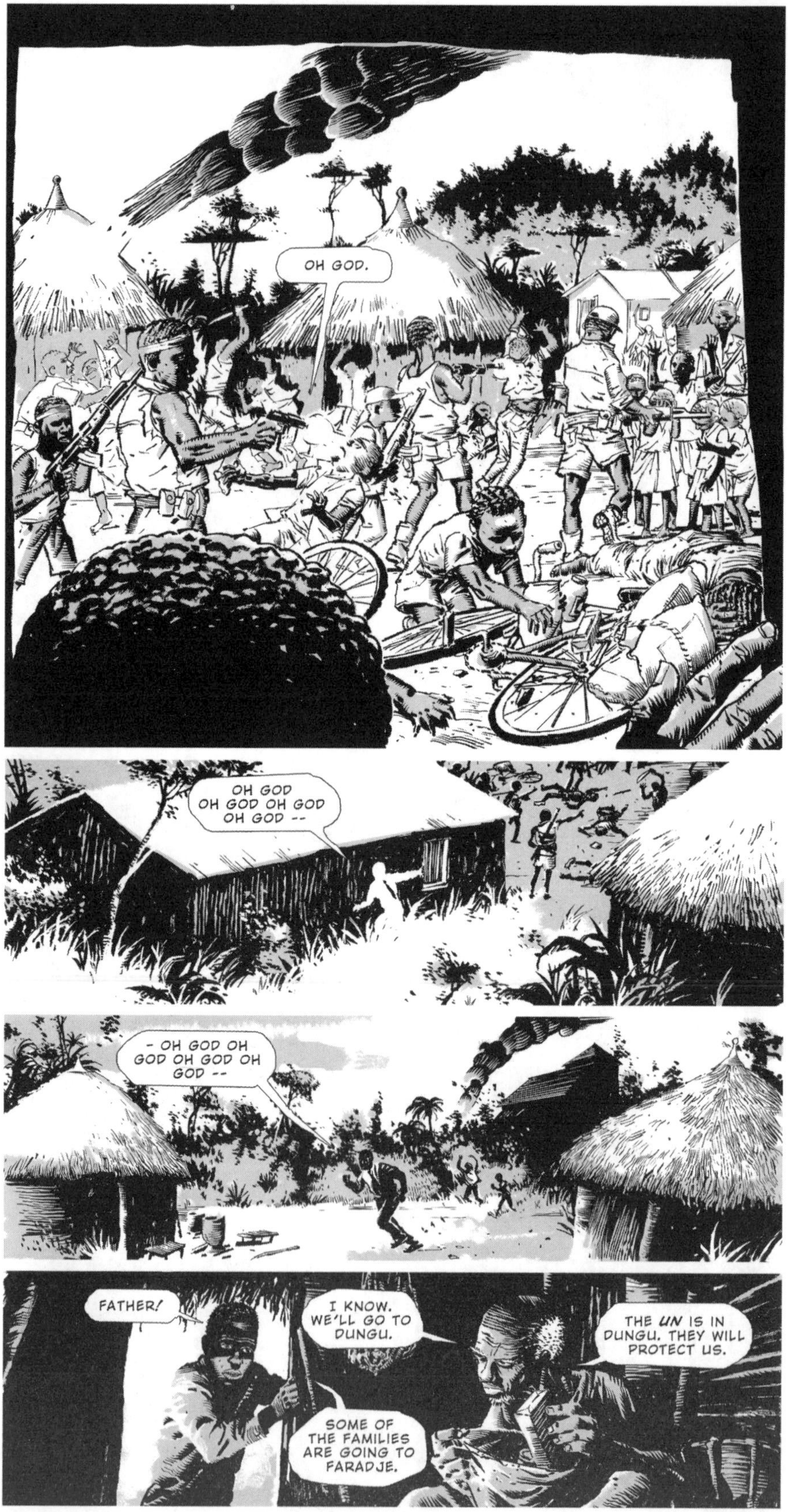
OH GOD.
OH GOD OH GOD OH GOD OH GOD --
- OH GOD OH GOD OH GOD OH GOD --
FATHER!
I KNOW. WE'LL GO TO DUNGU.
SOME OF THE FAMILIES ARE GOING TO FARADJE.
THE *UN* IS IN DUNGU. THEY WILL PROTECT US.

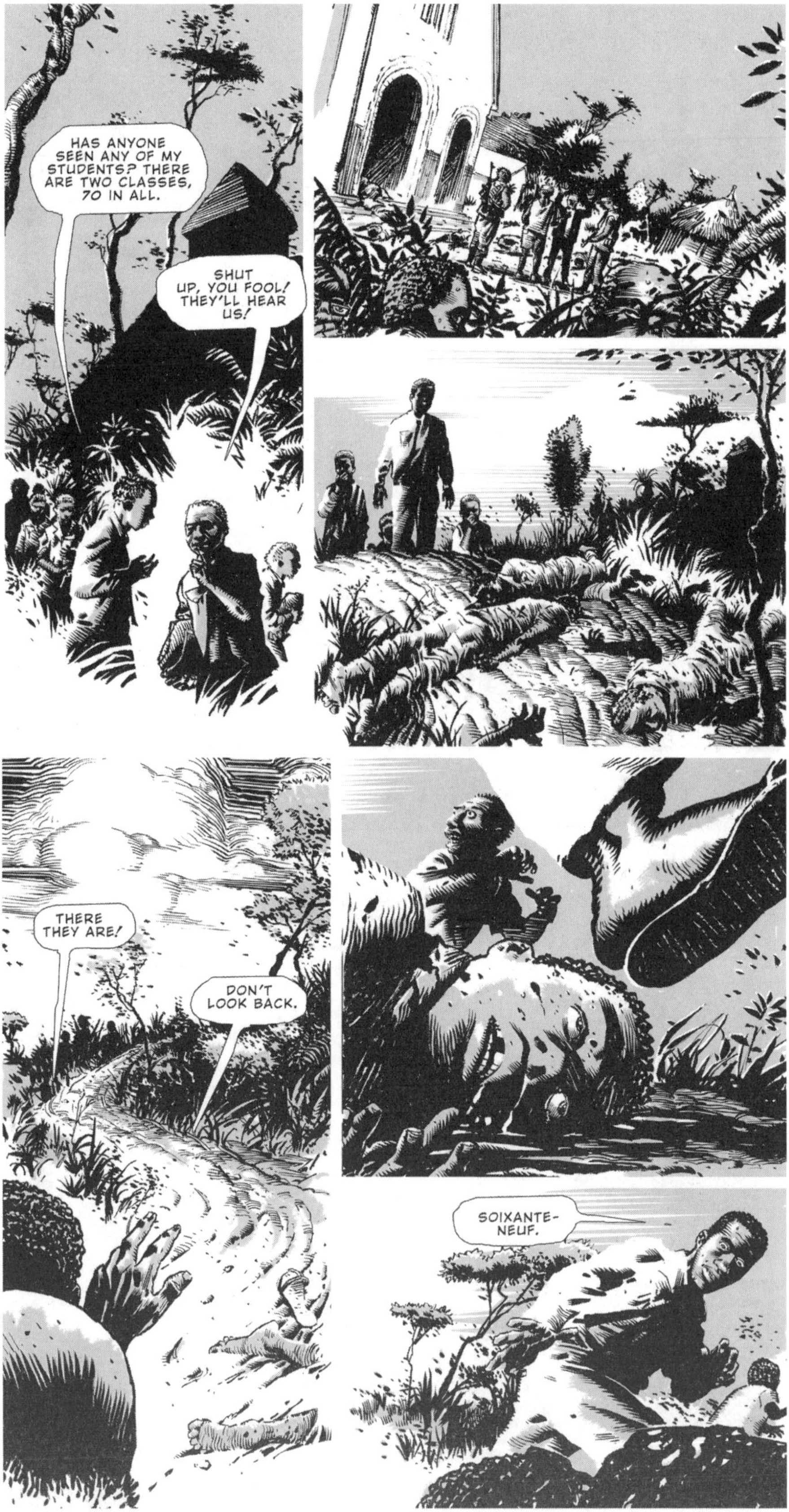
HAS ANYONE SEEN ANY OF MY STUDENTS? THERE ARE TWO CLASSES, 70 IN ALL.
SHUT UP, YOU FOOL! THEY'LL HEAR US!
THERE THEY ARE!
DON'T LOOK BACK.
SOIXANTE-NEUF.

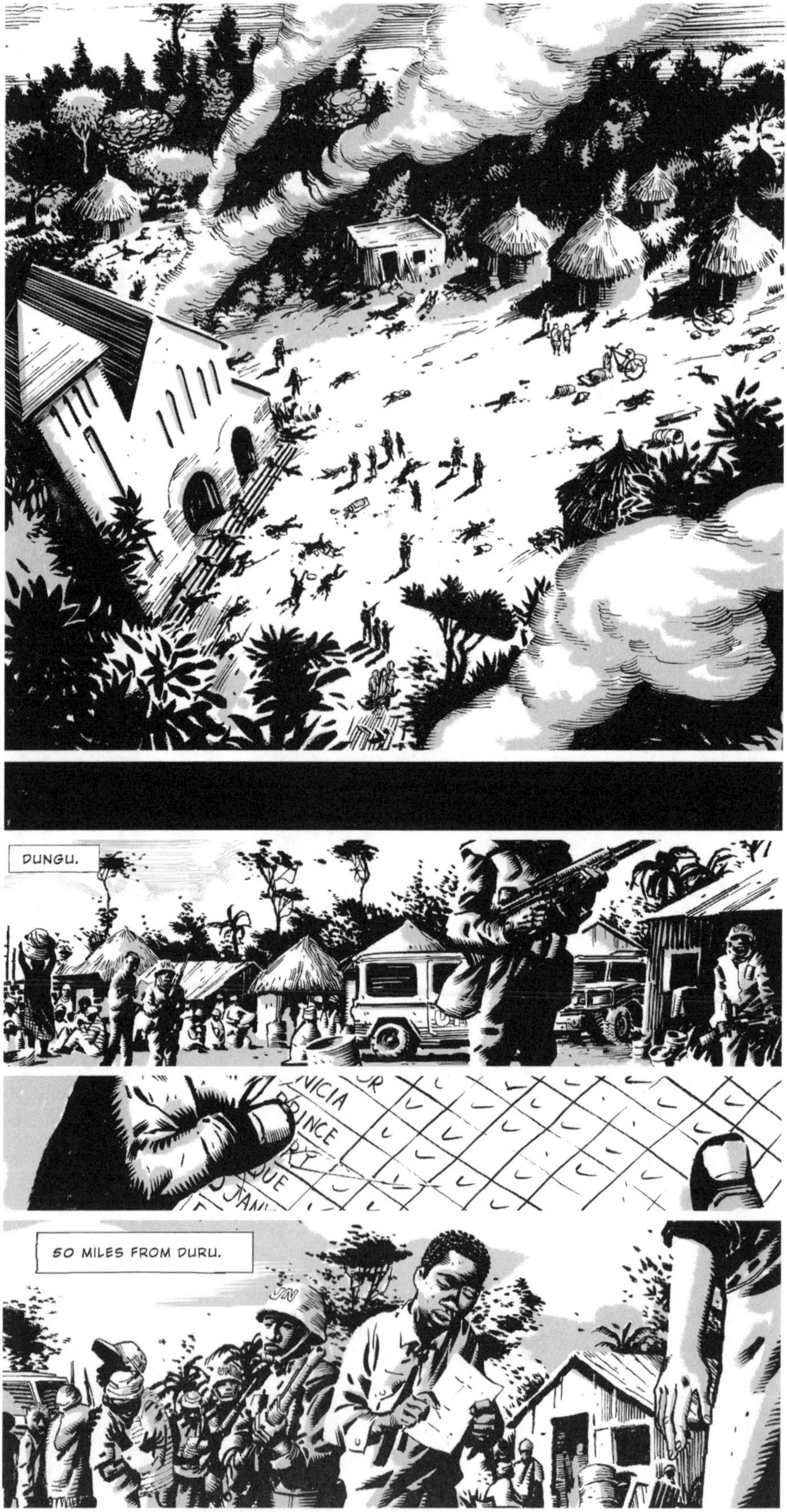
DUNGU.
50 MILES FROM DURU.

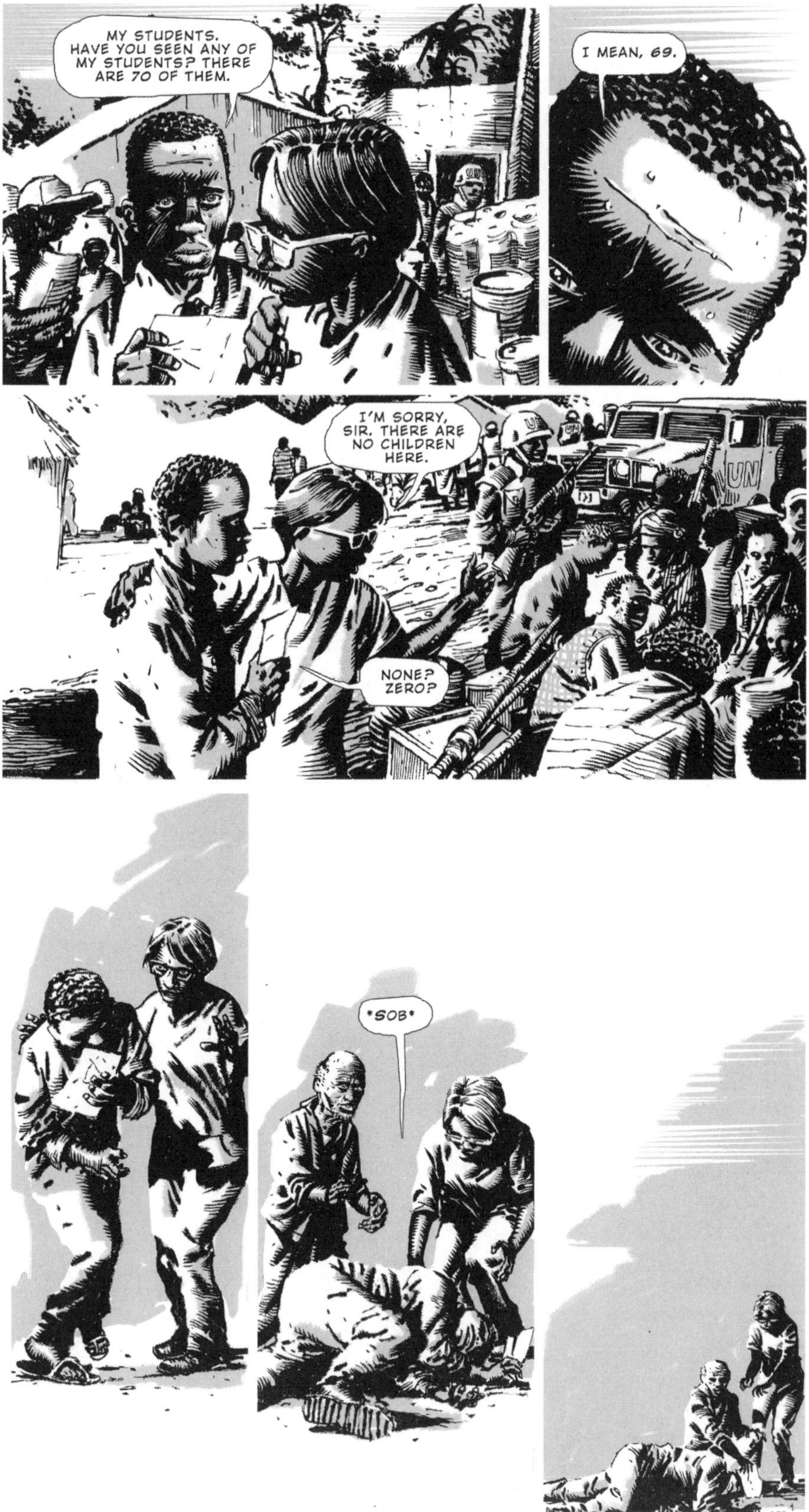
MY STUDENTS. HAVE YOU SEEN ANY OF MY STUDENTS? THERE ARE 70 OF THEM.
I MEAN, 69.
I'M SORRY, SIR. THERE ARE NO CHILDREN HERE.
NONE? ZERO?
SOB

CHAPTER TWO: THE PRIEST

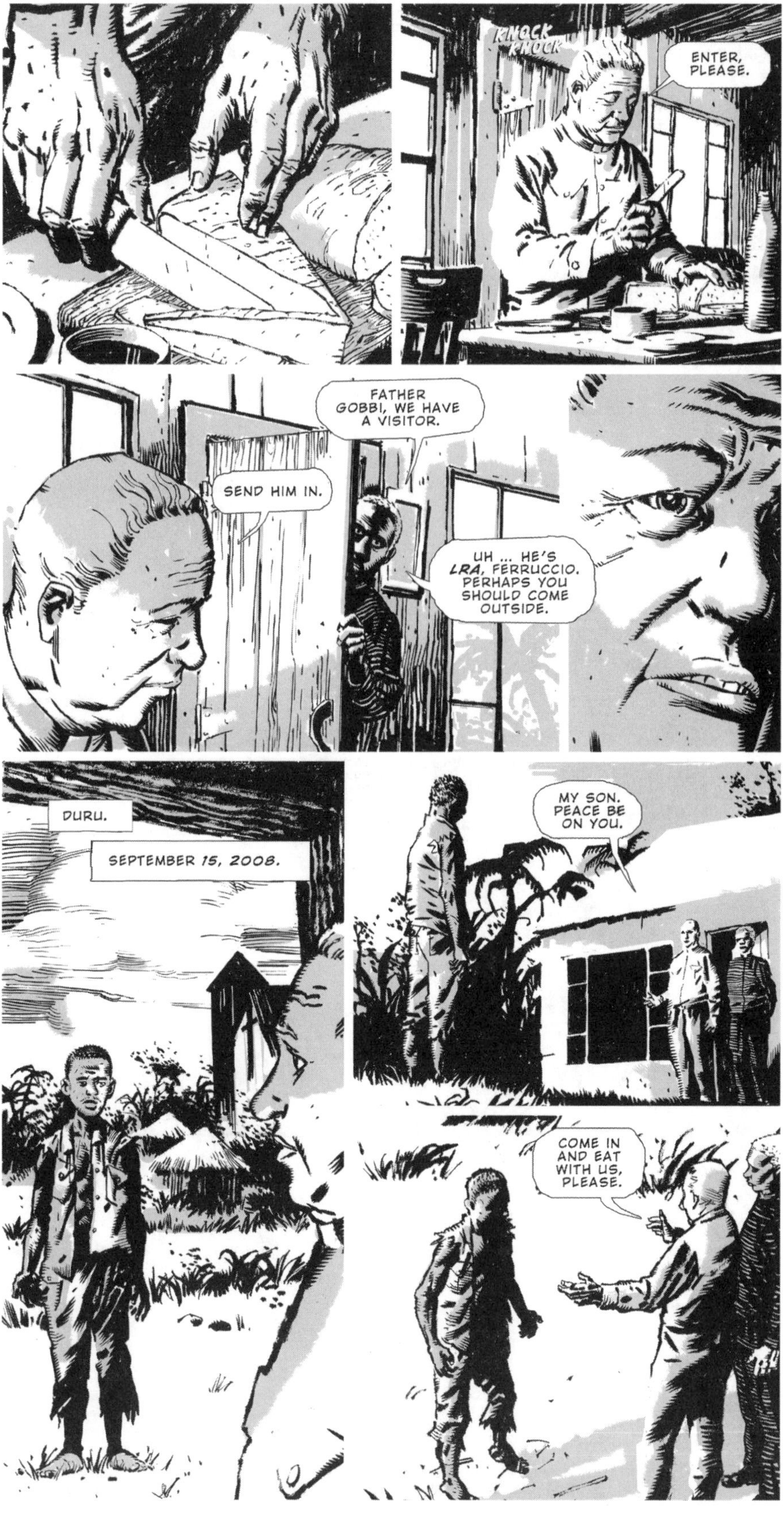
KNOCK KNOCK
ENTER, PLEASE.
FATHER GOBBI, WE HAVE A VISITOR.
SEND HIM IN.
UH ... HE'S LRA, FERRUCCIO. PERHAPS YOU SHOULD COME OUTSIDE.
DURU.
SEPTEMBER 15, 2008.
MY SON. PEACE BE ON YOU.
COME IN AND EAT WITH US, PLEASE.

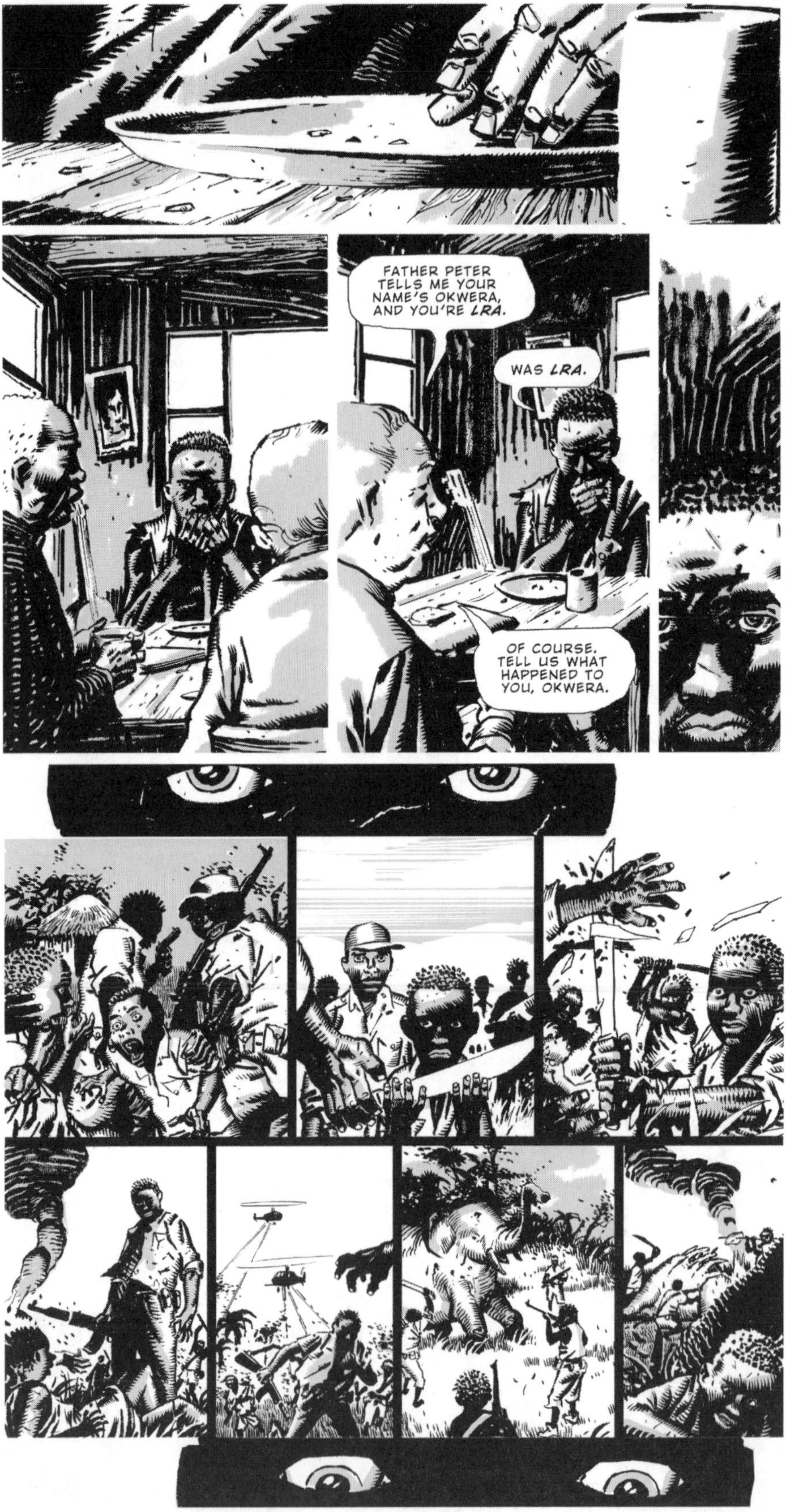
FATHER PETER TELLS ME YOUR NAME'S OKWERA, AND YOU'RE LRA.
WAS LRA.
OF COURSE. TELL US WHAT HAPPENED TO YOU, OKWERA.

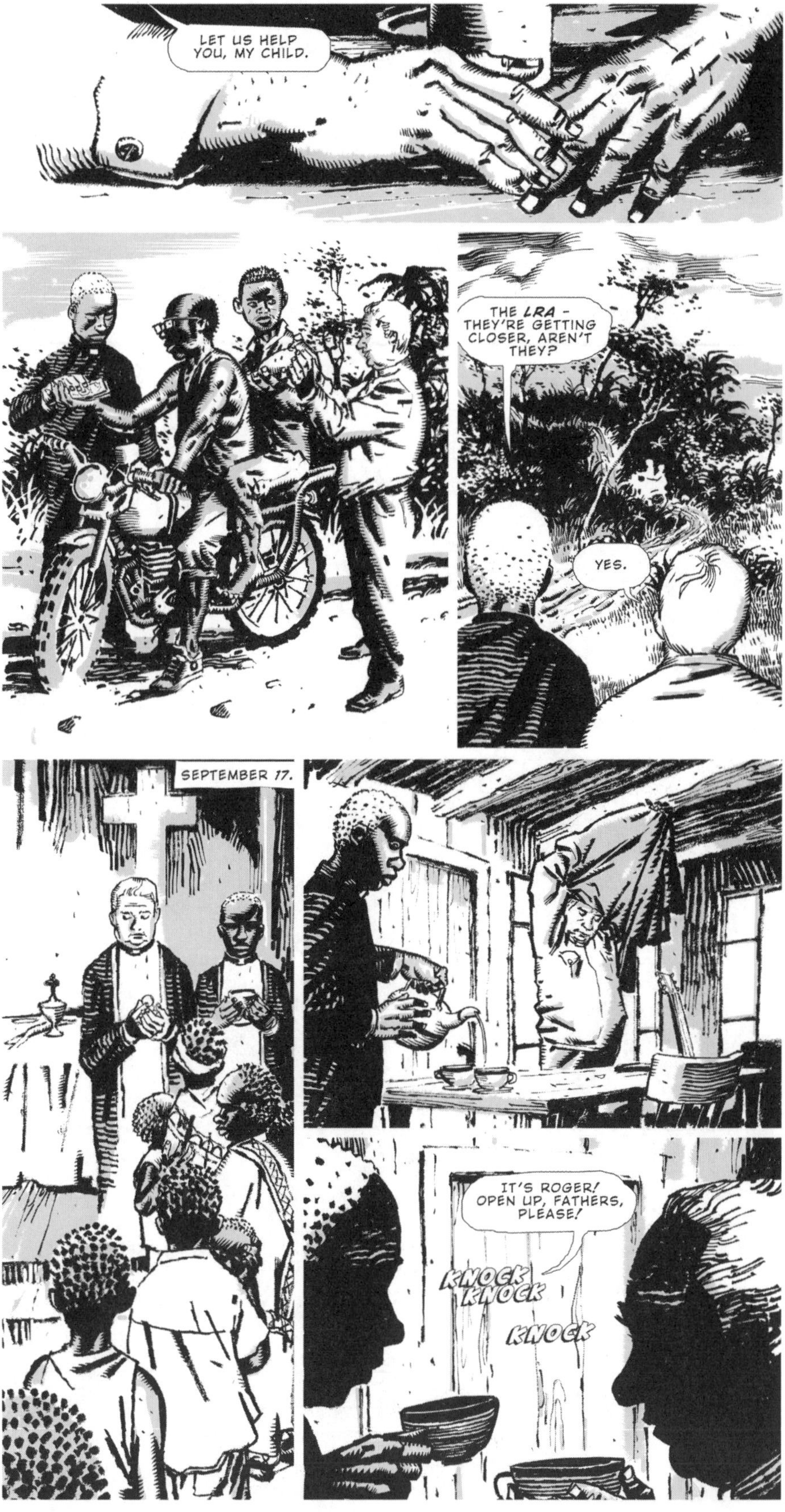
LET US HELP YOU, MY CHILD.
THE *LRA* - THEY'RE GETTING CLOSER, AREN'T THEY?
YES.
SEPTEMBER 17.
IT'S ROGER! OPEN UP, FATHERS, PLEASE!
KNOCK KNOCK
KNOCK

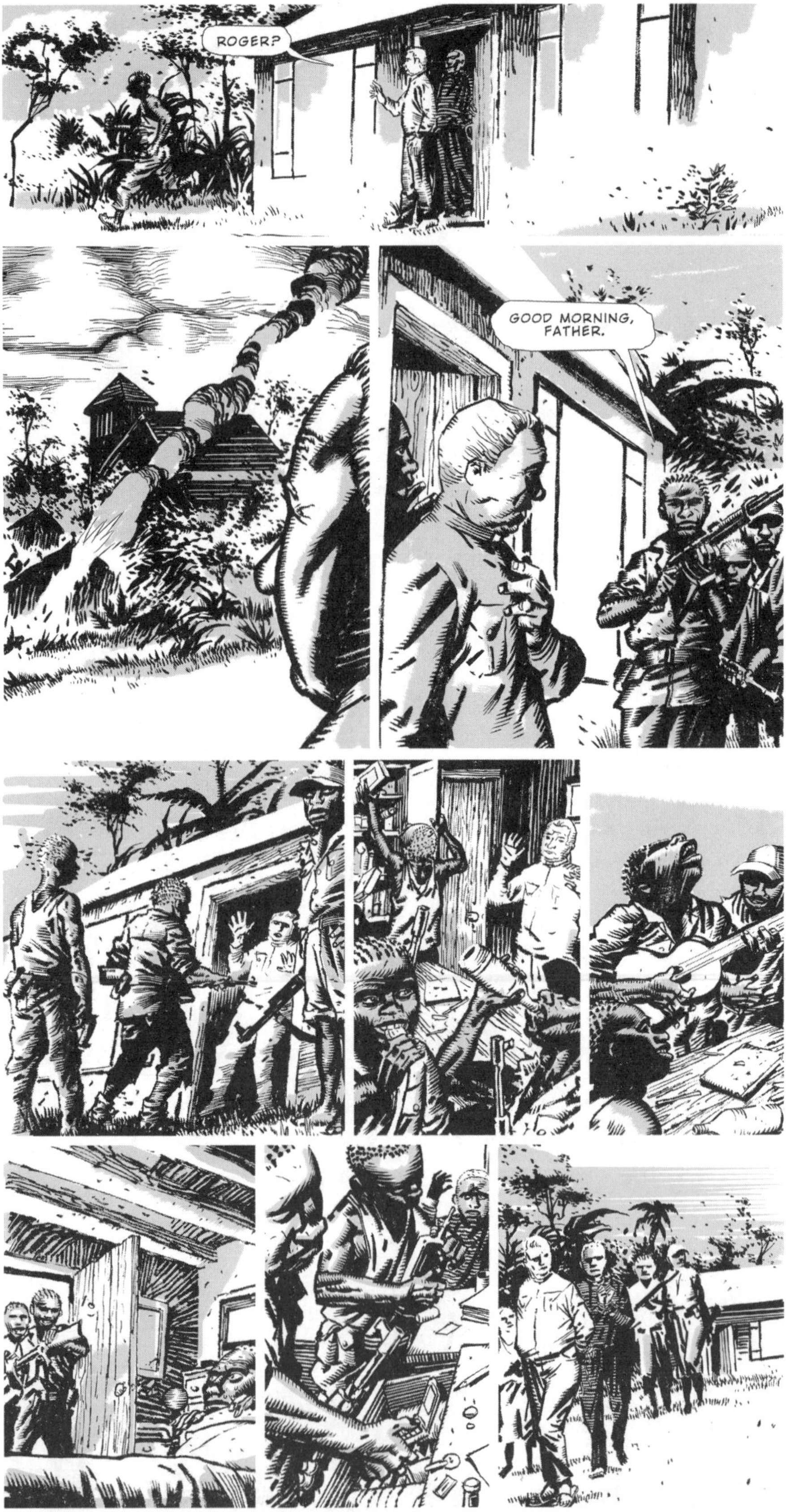
ROGER?
GOOD MORNING, FATHER.

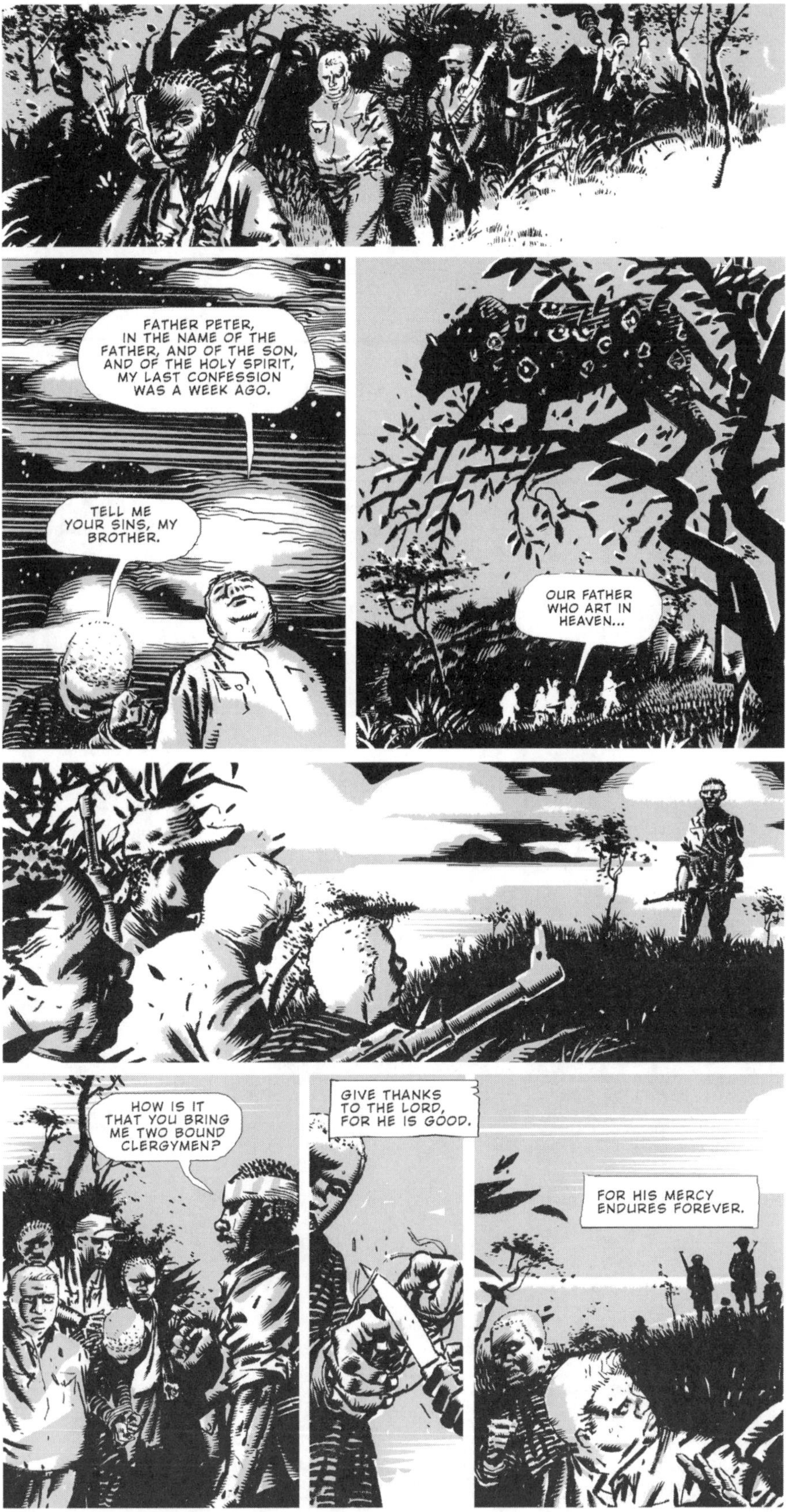
FATHER PETER, IN THE NAME OF THE FATHER, AND OF THE SON, AND OF THE HOLY SPIRIT, MY LAST CONFESSION WAS A WEEK AGO.
TELL ME YOUR SINS, MY BROTHER.
OUR FATHER WHO ART IN HEAVEN...
HOW IS IT THAT YOU BRING ME TWO BOUND CLERGYMEN?
GIVE THANKS TO THE LORD, FOR HE IS GOOD.
FOR HIS MERCY ENDURES FOREVER.

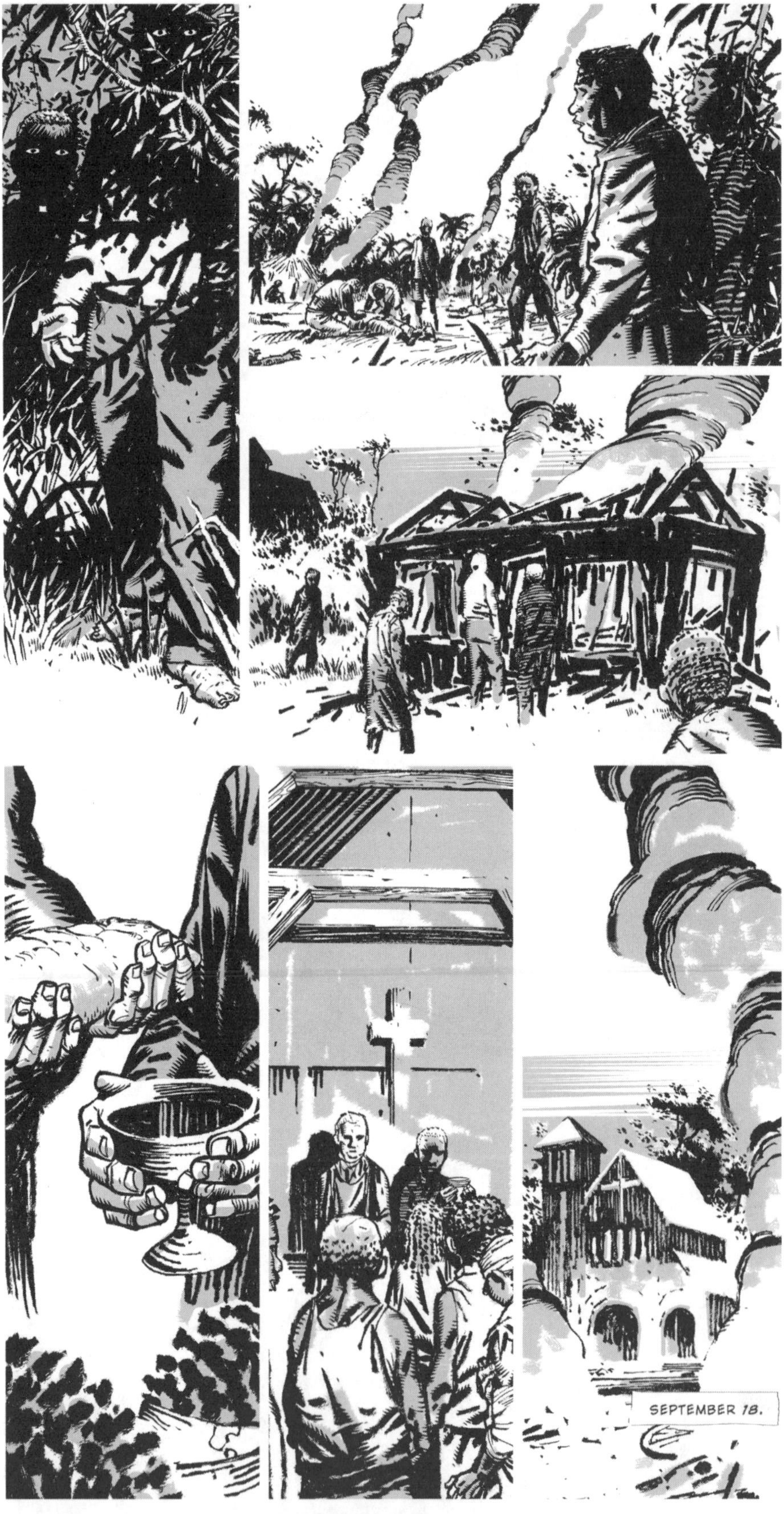
SEPTEMBER 18.

CHAPTER THREE: JOSEPH KONY

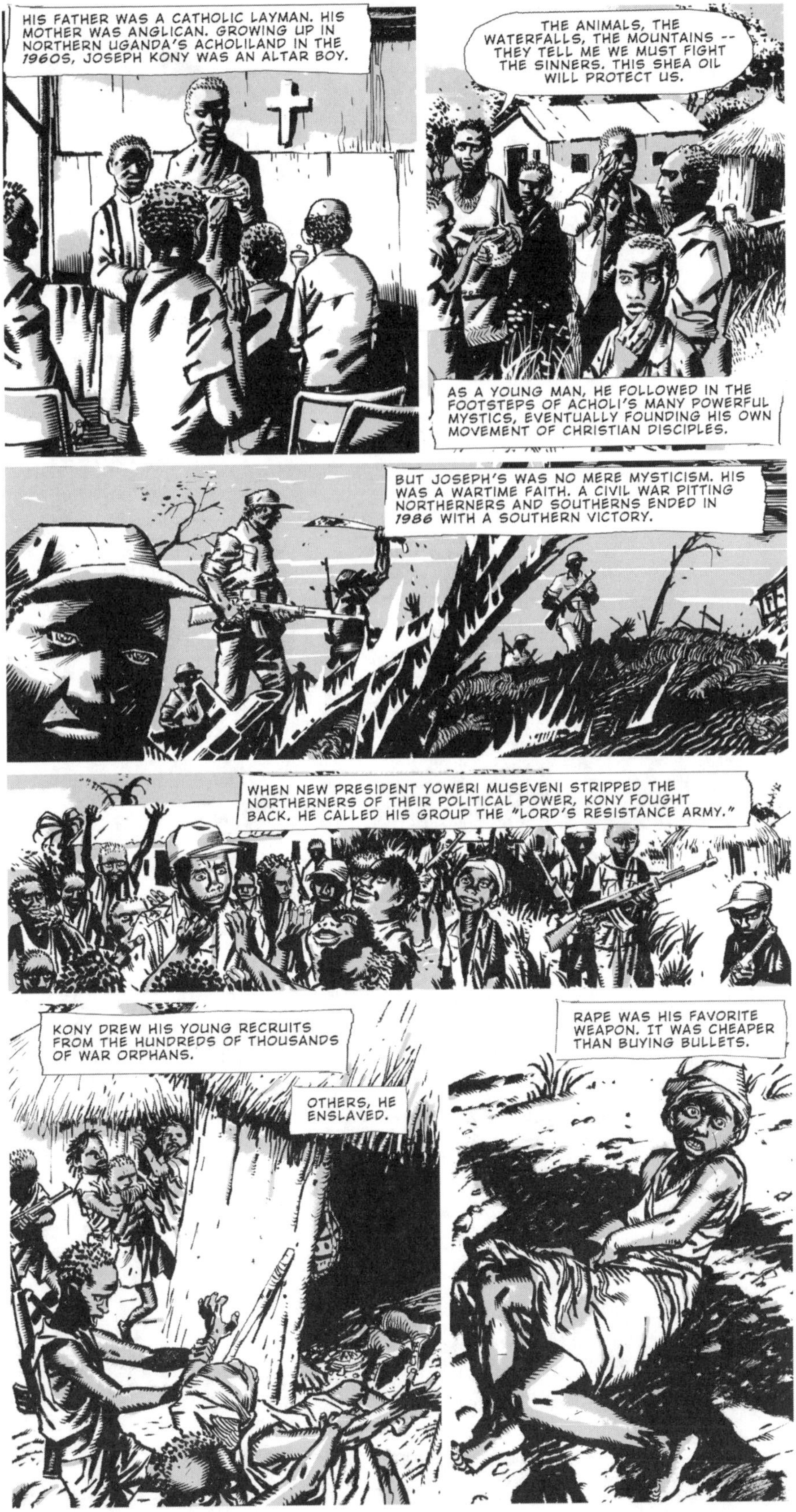
HIS FATHER WAS A CATHOLIC LAYMAN. HIS MOTHER WAS ANGLICAN. GROWING UP IN NORTHERN UGANDA'S ACHOLILAND IN THE 1960S, JOSEPH KONY WAS AN ALTAR BOY.
THE ANIMALS, THE WATERFALLS, THE MOUNTAINS -- THEY TELL ME WE MUST FIGHT THE SINNERS. THIS SHEA OIL WILL PROTECT US.
AS A YOUNG MAN, HE FOLLOWED IN THE FOOTSTEPS OF ACHOLI'S MANY POWERFUL MYSTICS, EVENTUALLY FOUNDING HIS OWN MOVEMENT OF CHRISTIAN DISCIPLES.
BUT JOSEPH'S WAS NO MERE MYSTICISM. HIS WAS A WARTIME FAITH. A CIVIL WAR PITTING NORTHERNERS AND SOUTHERNS ENDED IN 1986 WITH A SOUTHERN VICTORY.
WHEN NEW PRESIDENT YOWERI MUSEVENI STRIPPED THE NORTHERNERS OF THEIR POLITICAL POWER, KONY FOUGHT BACK. HE CALLED HIS GROUP THE "LORD'S RESISTANCE ARMY."
KONY DREW HIS YOUNG RECRUITS FROM THE HUNDREDS OF THOUSANDS OF WAR ORPHANS.
OTHERS, HE ENSLAVED.
RAPE WAS HIS FAVORITE WEAPON. IT WAS CHEAPER THAN BUYING BULLETS.

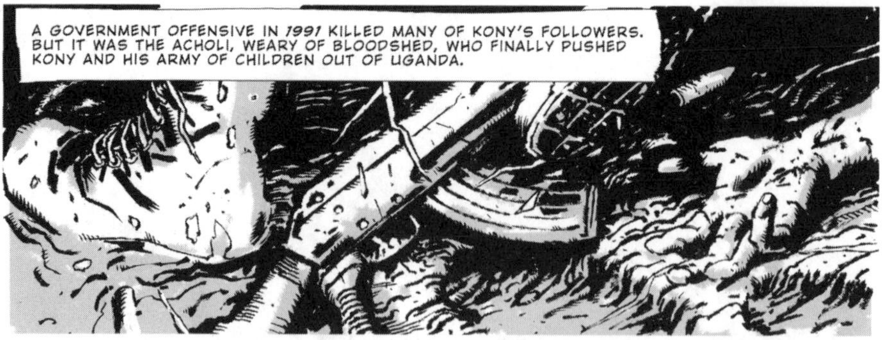
A GOVERNMENT OFFENSIVE IN 1991 KILLED MANY OF KONY'S FOLLOWERS. BUT IT WAS THE ACHOLI, WEARY OF BLOODSHED, WHO FINALLY PUSHED KONY AND HIS ARMY OF CHILDREN OUT OF UGANDA.

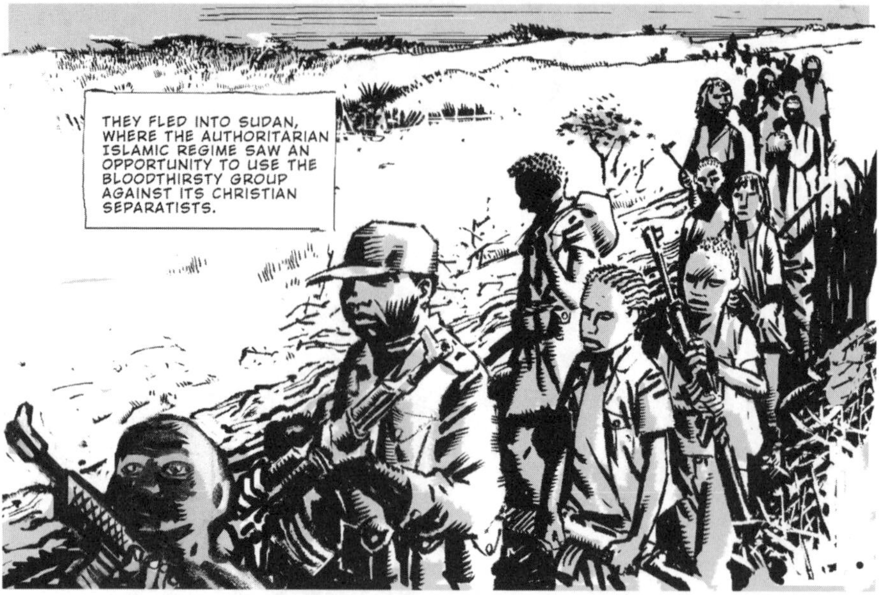
THEY FLED INTO SUDAN, WHERE THE AUTHORITARIAN ISLAMIC REGIME SAW AN OPPORTUNITY TO USE THE BLOODTHIRSTY GROUP AGAINST ITS CHRISTIAN SEPARATISTS.

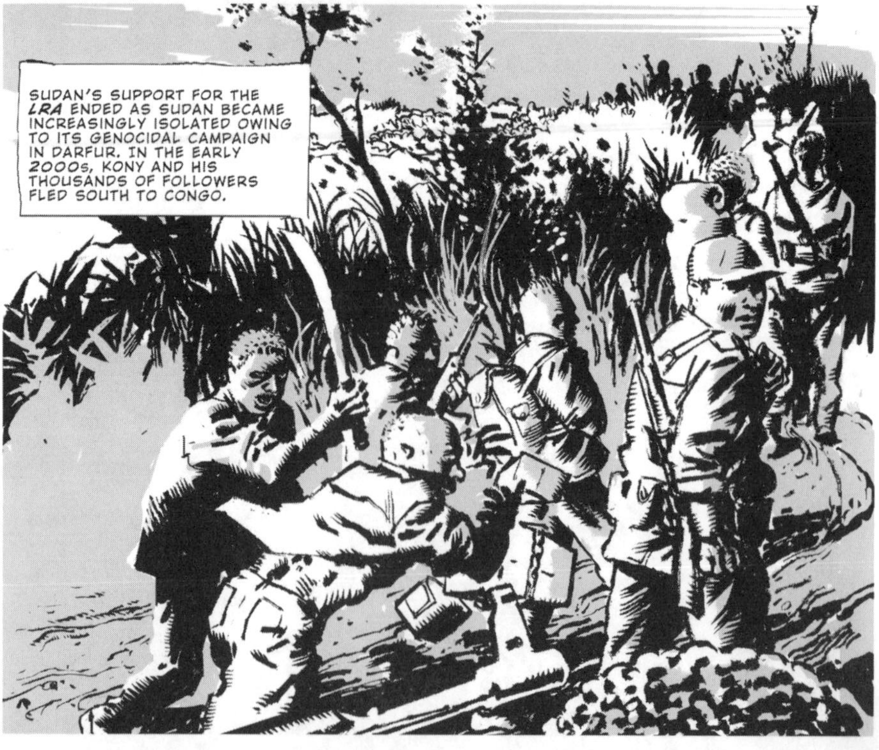
SUDAN'S SUPPORT FOR THE LRA ENDED AS SUDAN BECAME INCREASINGLY ISOLATED OWING TO ITS GENOCIDAL CAMPAIGN IN DARFUR. IN THE EARLY 2000s, KONY AND HIS THOUSANDS OF FOLLOWERS FLED SOUTH TO CONGO.

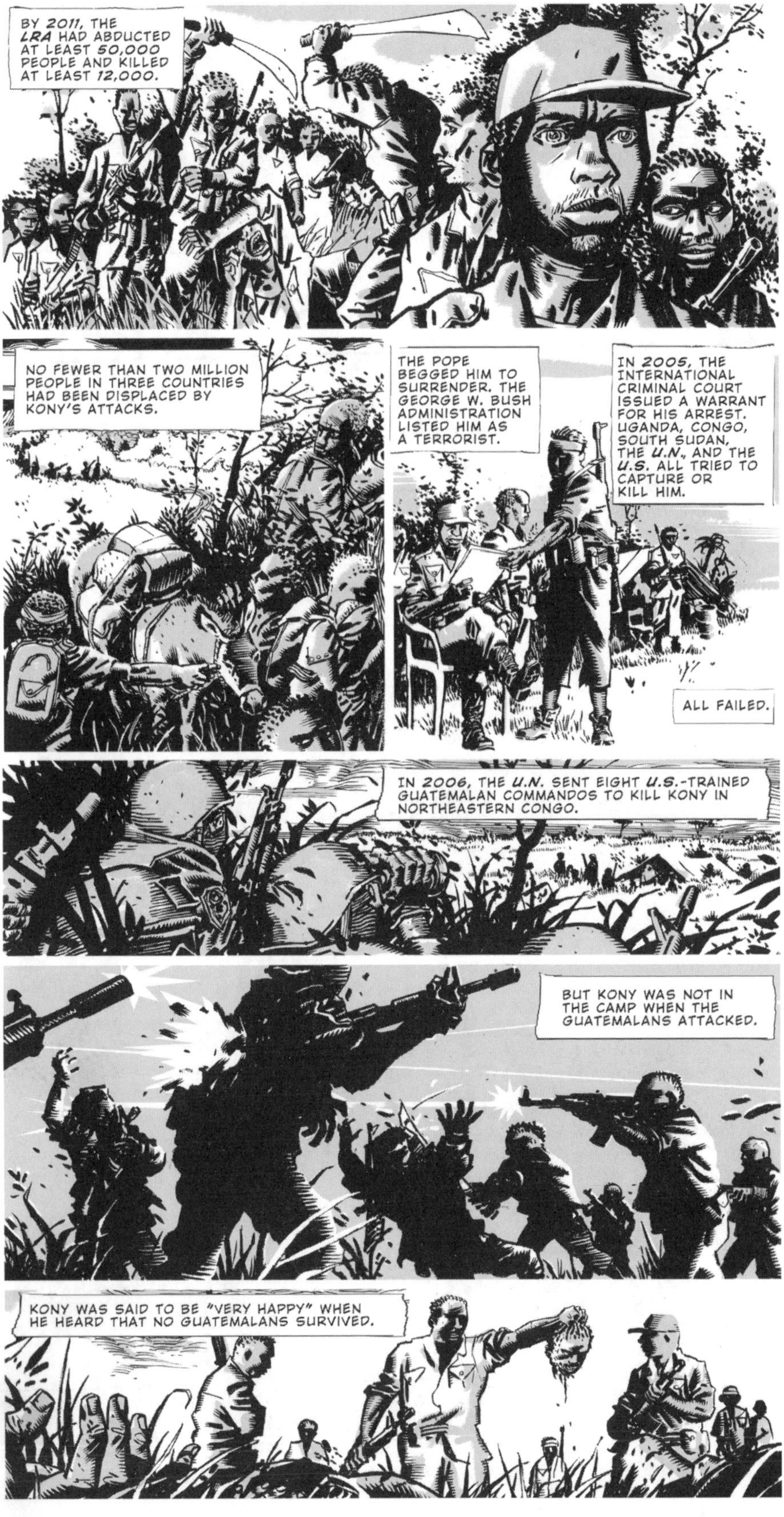
BY 2011, THE LRA HAD ABDUCTED AT LEAST 50,000 PEOPLE AND KILLED AT LEAST 12,000.
NO FEWER THAN TWO MILLION PEOPLE IN THREE COUNTRIES HAD BEEN DISPLACED BY KONY'S ATTACKS.
THE POPE BEGGED HIM TO SURRENDER. THE GEORGE W. BUSH ADMINISTRATION LISTED HIM AS A TERRORIST.
IN 2005, THE INTERNATIONAL CRIMINAL COURT ISSUED A WARRANT FOR HIS ARREST. UGANDA, CONGO, SOUTH SUDAN, THE U.N., AND THE U.S. ALL TRIED TO CAPTURE OR KILL HIM.
ALL FAILED.
IN 2006, THE U.N. SENT EIGHT U.S.-TRAINED GUATEMALAN COMMANDOS TO KILL KONY IN NORTHEASTERN CONGO.
BUT KONY WAS NOT IN THE CAMP WHEN THE GUATEMALANS ATTACKED.
KONY WAS SAID TO BE "VERY HAPPY" WHEN HE HEARD THAT NO GUATEMALANS SURVIVED.

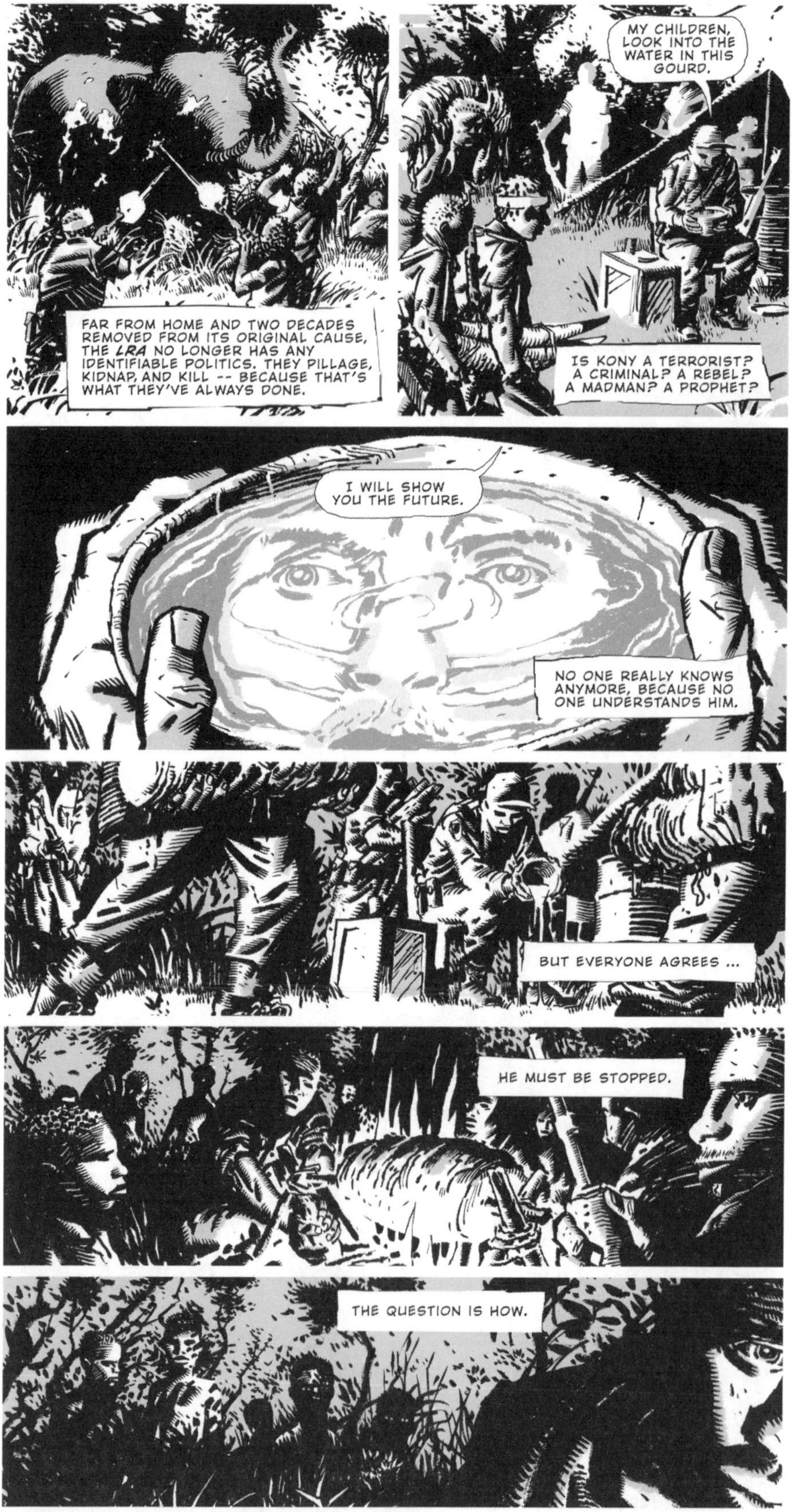
FAR FROM HOME AND TWO DECADES REMOVED FROM ITS ORIGINAL CAUSE, THE *LRA* NO LONGER HAS ANY IDENTIFIABLE POLITICS. THEY PILLAGE, KIDNAP, AND KILL -- BECAUSE THAT'S WHAT THEY'VE ALWAYS DONE.
MY CHILDREN, LOOK INTO THE WATER IN THIS GOURD.
IS KONY A TERRORIST? A CRIMINAL? A REBEL? A MADMAN? A PROPHET?
I WILL SHOW YOU THE FUTURE.
NO ONE REALLY KNOWS ANYMORE, BECAUSE NO ONE UNDERSTANDS HIM.
BUT EVERYONE AGREES ...
HE MUST BE STOPPED.
THE QUESTION IS HOW.

CHAPTER FOUR:
THE SOLDIERS

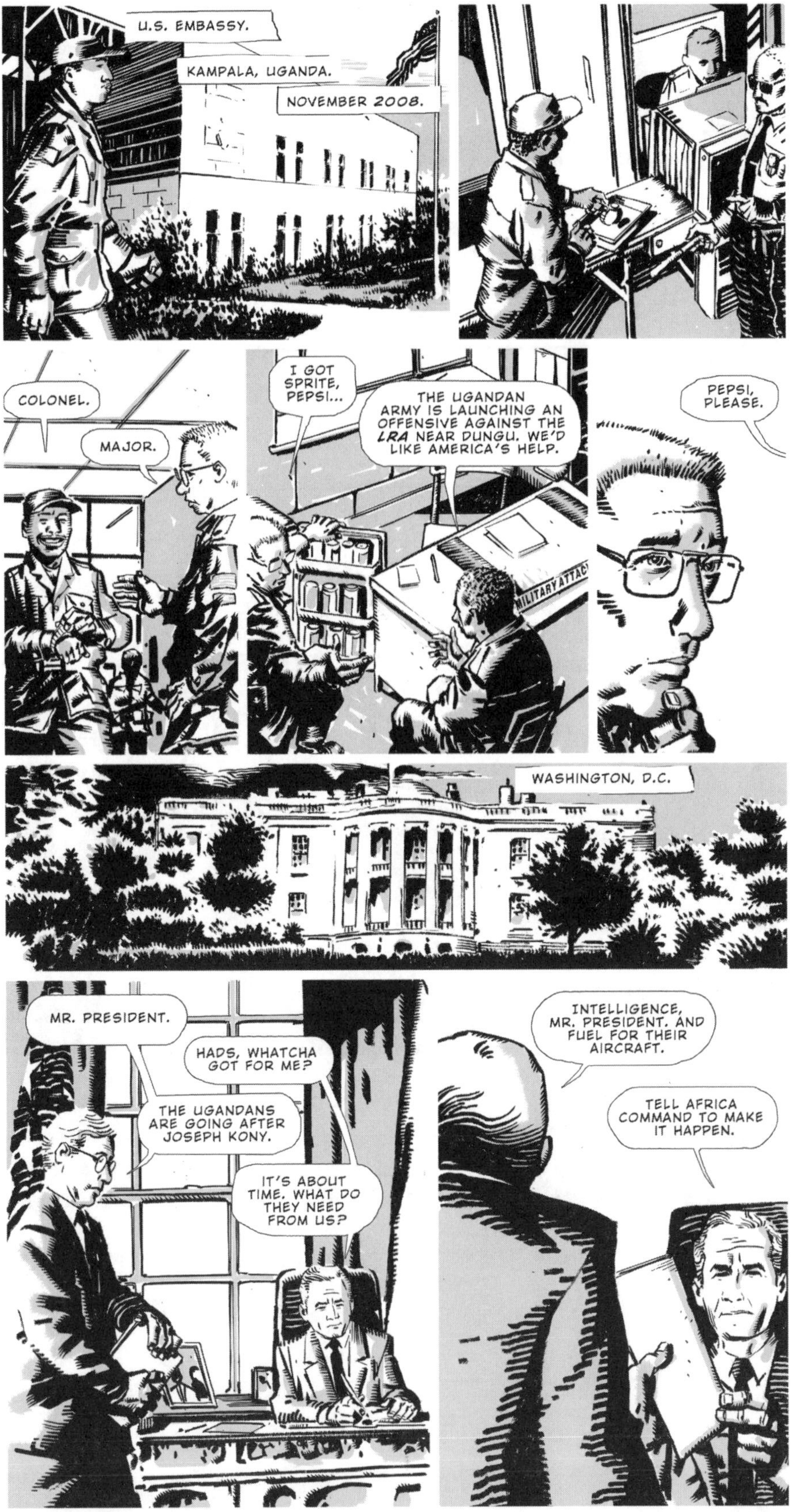
U.S. EMBASSY.
KAMPALA, UGANDA.
NOVEMBER 2008.
COLONEL.
MAJOR.
I GOT SPRITE, PEPSI...
THE UGANDAN ARMY IS LAUNCHING AN OFFENSIVE AGAINST THE *LRA* NEAR DUNGU. WE'D LIKE AMERICA'S HELP.
MILITARY ATTACH
PEPSI, PLEASE.
WASHINGTON, D.C.
MR. PRESIDENT.
HADS, WHATCHA GOT FOR ME?
THE UGANDANS ARE GOING AFTER JOSEPH KONY.
IT'S ABOUT TIME. WHAT DO THEY NEED FROM US?
INTELLIGENCE, MR. PRESIDENT. AND FUEL FOR THEIR AIRCRAFT.
TELL AFRICA COMMAND TO MAKE IT HAPPEN.

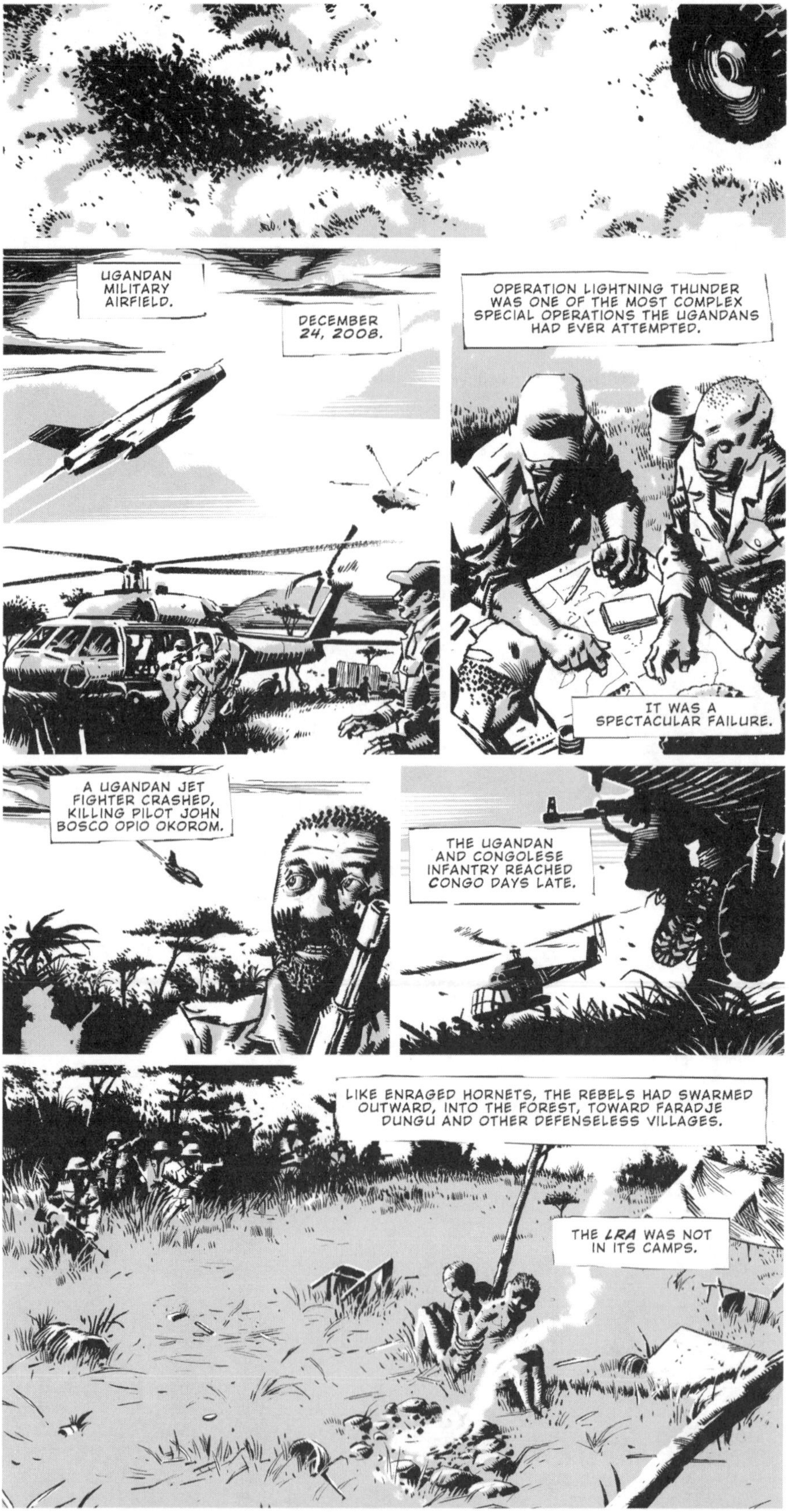

UGANDAN MILITARY AIRFIELD.
DECEMBER 24, 2008.
OPERATION LIGHTNING THUNDER WAS ONE OF THE MOST COMPLEX SPECIAL OPERATIONS THE UGANDANS HAD EVER ATTEMPTED.
IT WAS A SPECTACULAR FAILURE.
A UGANDAN JET FIGHTER CRASHED, KILLING PILOT JOHN BOSCO OPIO OKOROM.
THE UGANDAN AND CONGOLESE INFANTRY REACHED CONGO DAYS LATE.
LIKE ENRAGED HORNETS, THE REBELS HAD SWARMED OUTWARD, INTO THE FOREST, TOWARD FARADJE DUNGU AND OTHER DEFENSELESS VILLAGES.
THE *LRA* WAS NOT IN ITS CAMPS.

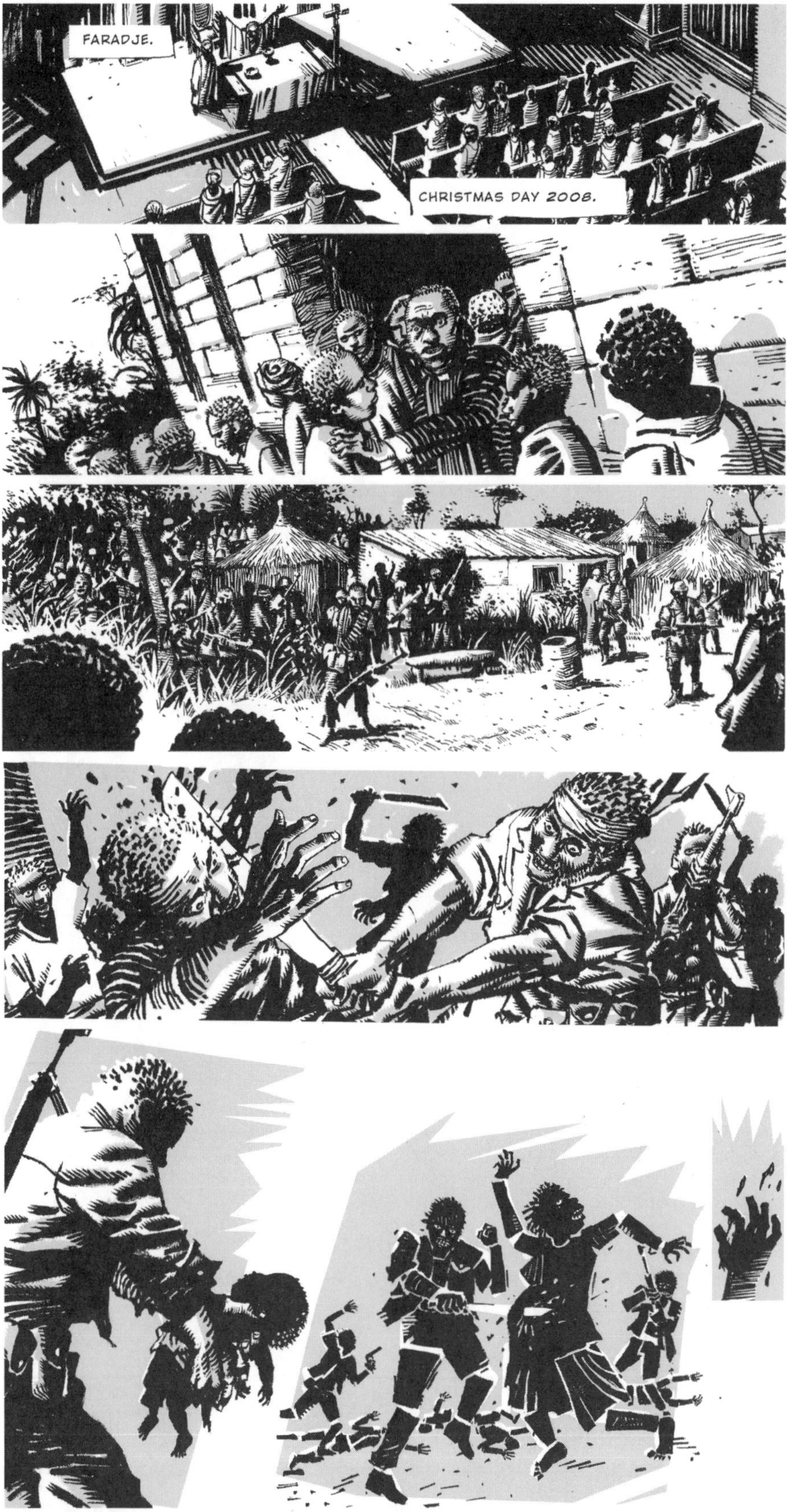
FARADJE.
CHRISTMAS DAY 2008.

CHAPTER FIVE:

THE GIRL
A PORTRAIT OF PATRICIA

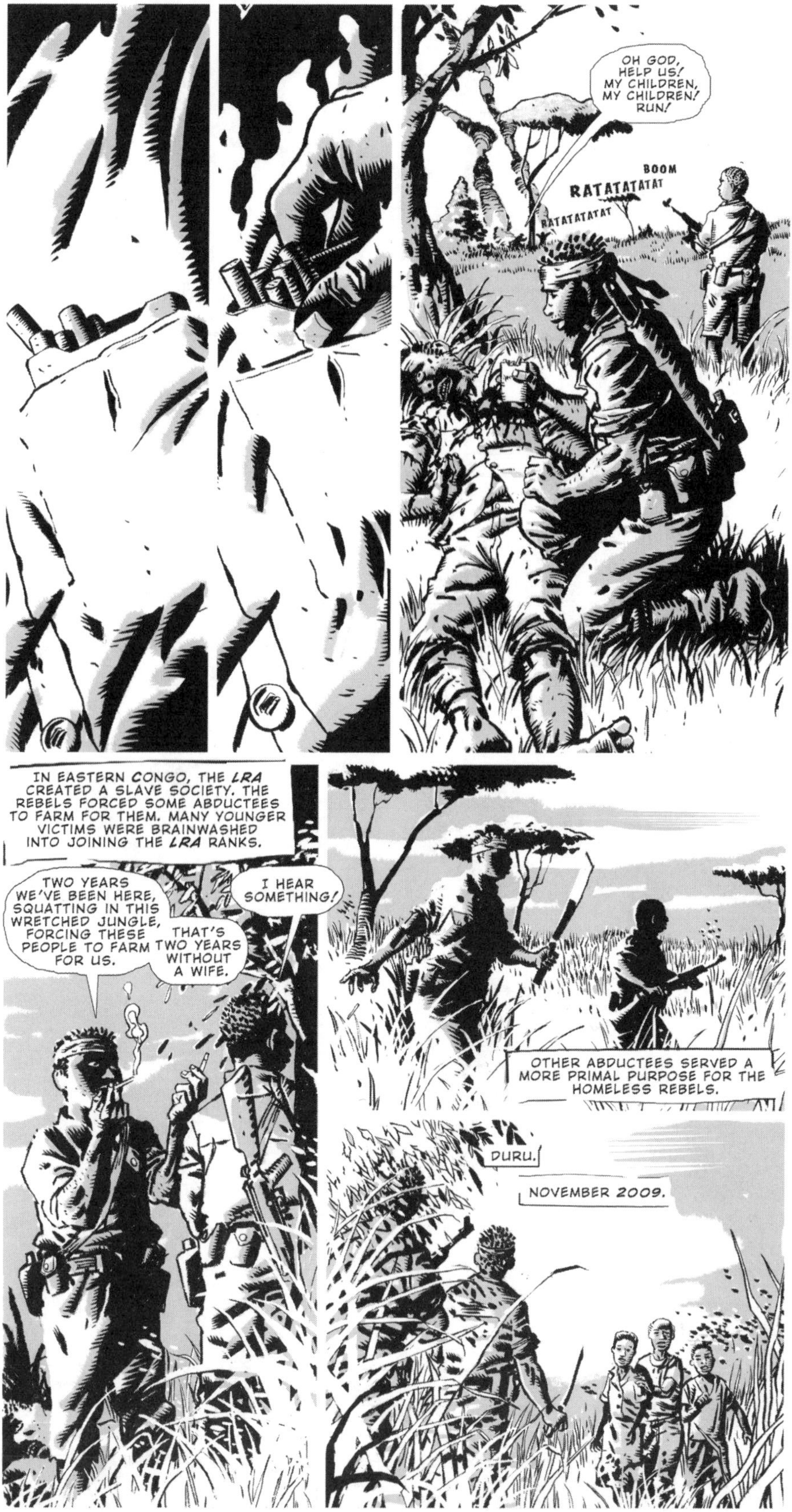

OH GOD, HELP US! MY CHILDREN, MY CHILDREN! RUN!
BOOM
RATATATATAT
RATATATATAT
IN EASTERN CONGO, THE LRA CREATED A SLAVE SOCIETY. THE REBELS FORCED SOME ABDUCTEES TO FARM FOR THEM. MANY YOUNGER VICTIMS WERE BRAINWASHED INTO JOINING THE LRA RANKS.
TWO YEARS WE'VE BEEN HERE, SQUATTING IN THIS WRETCHED JUNGLE, FORCING THESE PEOPLE TO FARM FOR US.
THAT'S TWO YEARS WITHOUT A WIFE.
I HEAR SOMETHING!
OTHER ABDUCTEES SERVED A MORE PRIMAL PURPOSE FOR THE HOMELESS REBELS.
DURU.
NOVEMBER 2009.

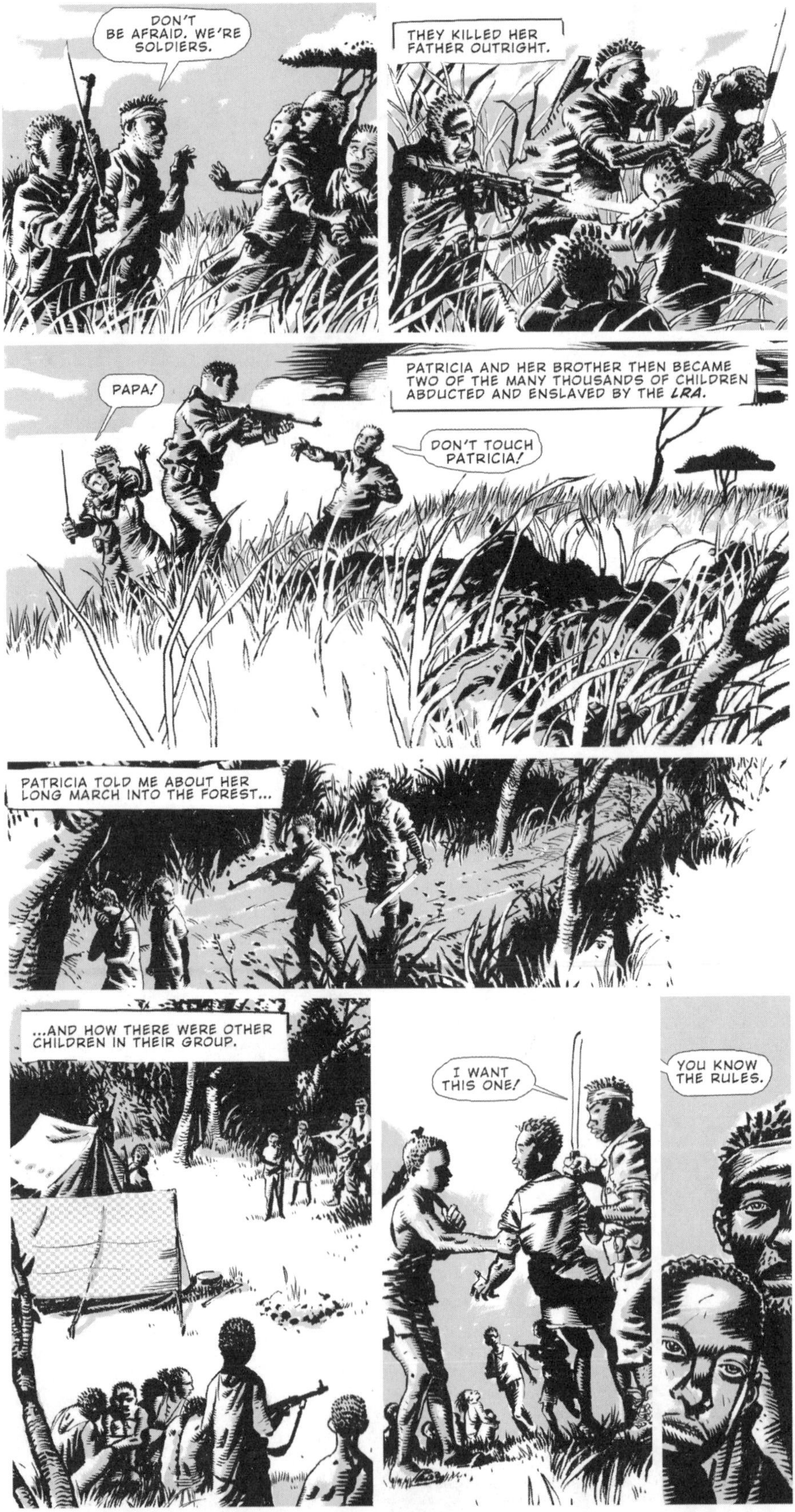
DON'T BE AFRAID. WE'RE SOLDIERS.
THEY KILLED HER FATHER OUTRIGHT.
PAPA!
PATRICIA AND HER BROTHER THEN BECAME TWO OF THE MANY THOUSANDS OF CHILDREN ABDUCTED AND ENSLAVED BY THE LRA.
DON'T TOUCH PATRICIA!
PATRICIA TOLD ME ABOUT HER LONG MARCH INTO THE FOREST...
...AND HOW THERE WERE OTHER CHILDREN IN THEIR GROUP.
I WANT THIS ONE!
YOU KNOW THE RULES.

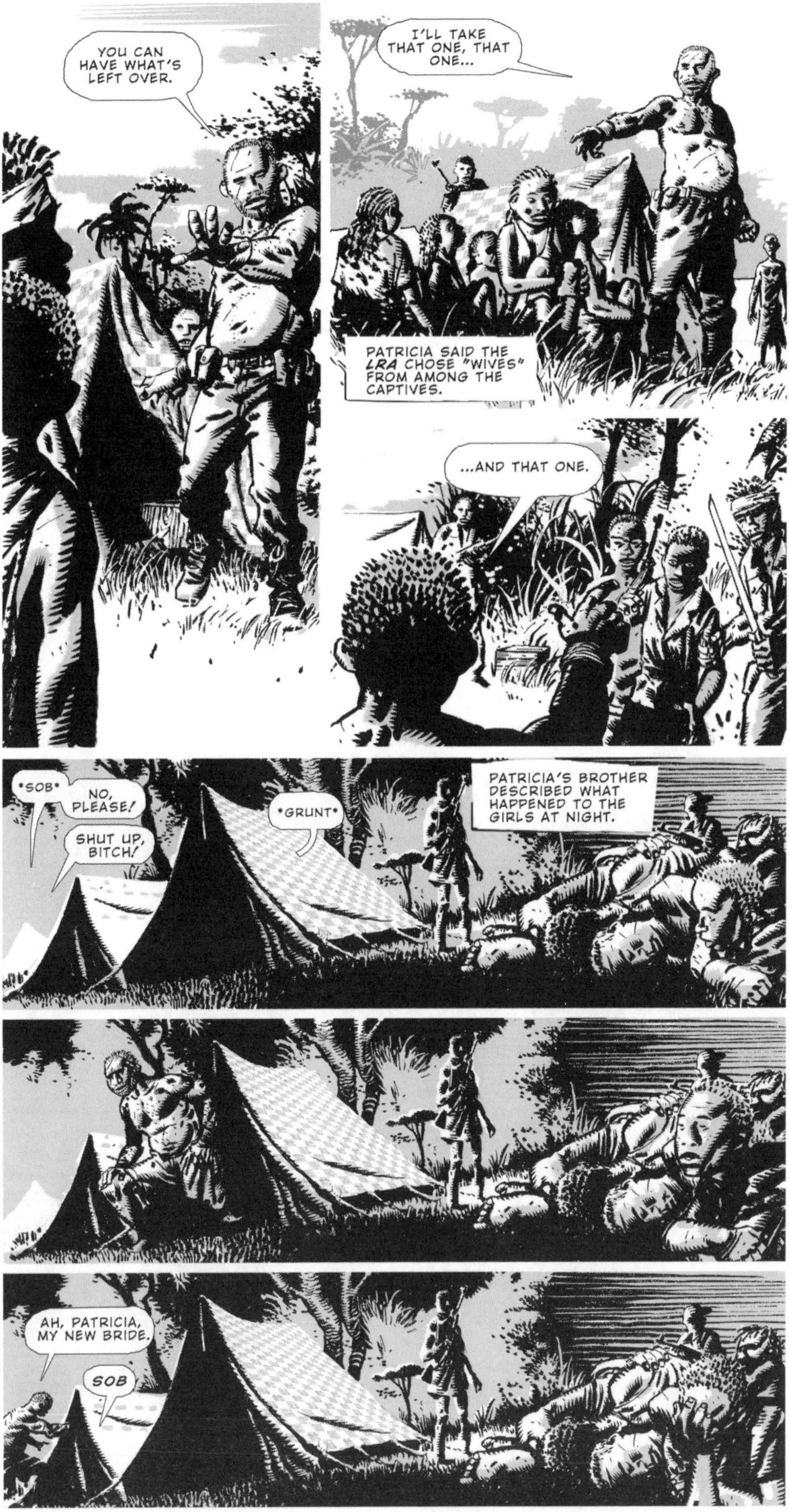
YOU CAN HAVE WHAT'S LEFT OVER.
I'LL TAKE THAT ONE, THAT ONE...
PATRICIA SAID THE LRA CHOSE "WIVES" FROM AMONG THE CAPTIVES.
...AND THAT ONE.
SOB
NO, PLEASE!
SHUT UP, BITCH!
GRUNT
PATRICIA'S BROTHER DESCRIBED WHAT HAPPENED TO THE GIRLS AT NIGHT.
AH, PATRICIA, MY NEW BRIDE.
SOB

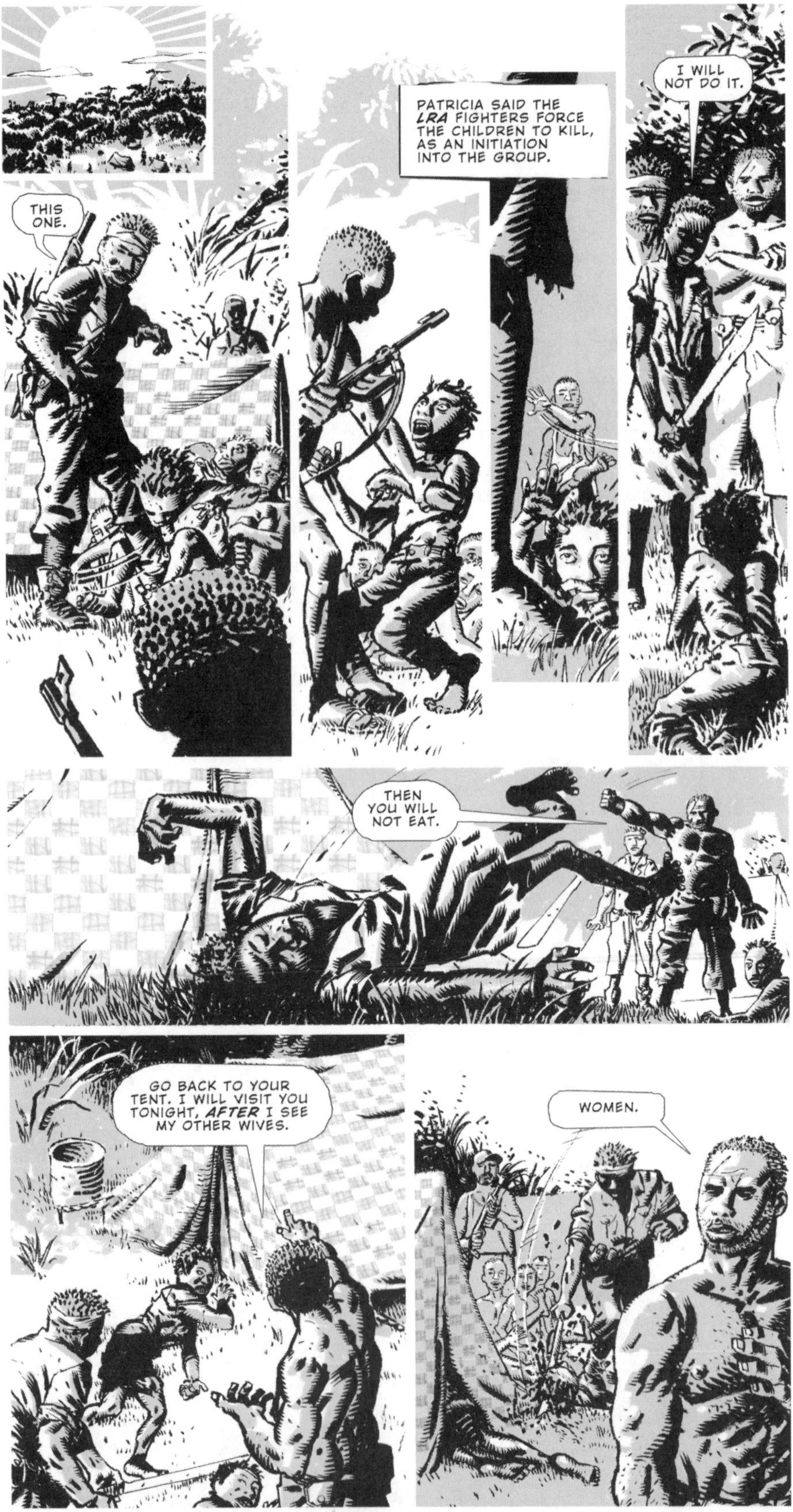
PATRICIA SAID THE LRA FIGHTERS FORCE THE CHILDREN TO KILL, AS AN INITIATION INTO THE GROUP.
THIS ONE.
I WILL NOT DO IT.
THEN YOU WILL NOT EAT.
GO BACK TO YOUR TENT. I WILL VISIT YOU TONIGHT, AFTER I SEE MY OTHER WIVES.
WOMEN.

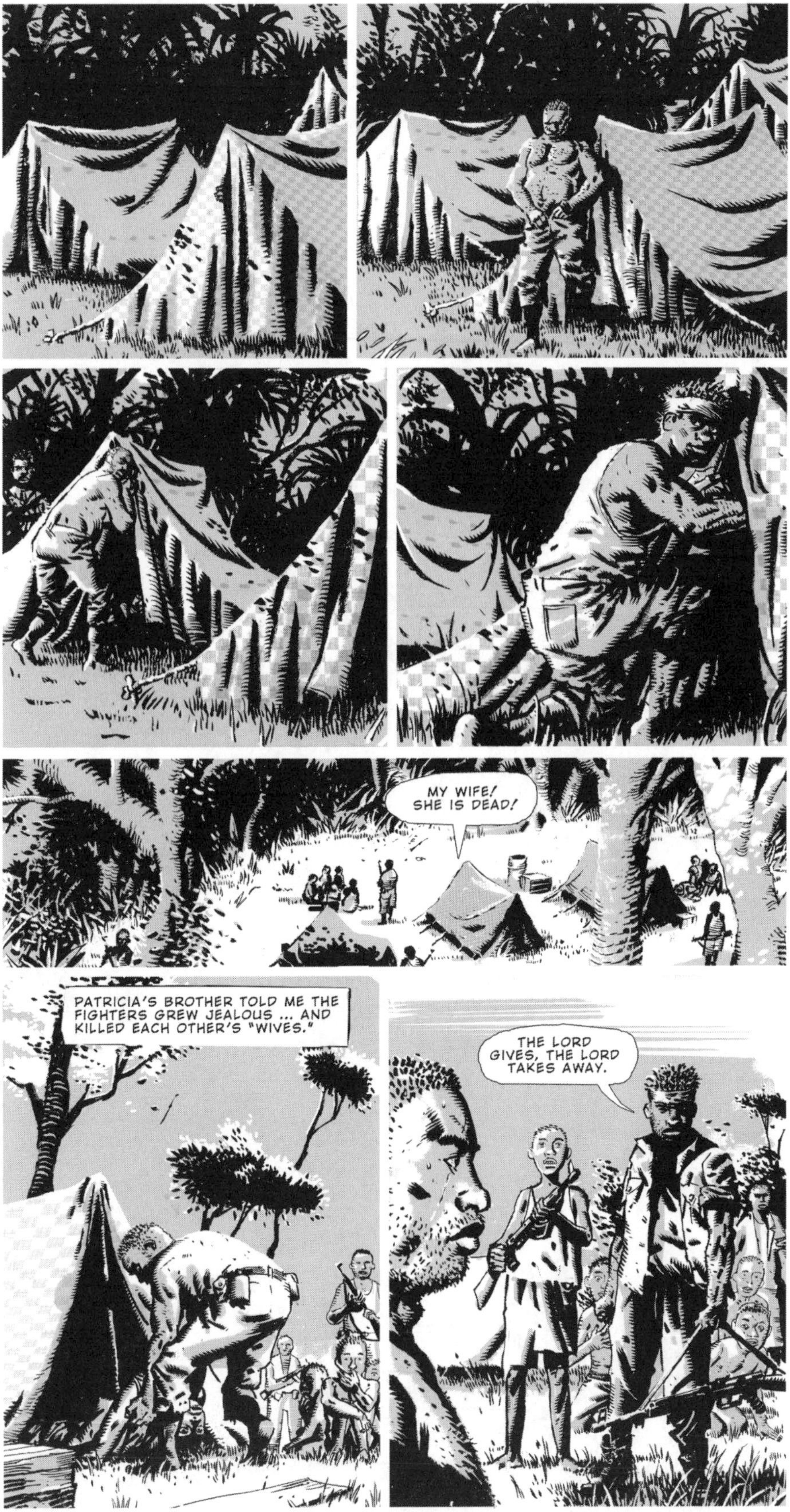
MY WIFE! SHE IS DEAD!
PATRICIA'S BROTHER TOLD ME THE FIGHTERS GREW JEALOUS ... AND KILLED EACH OTHER'S "WIVES."
THE LORD GIVES, THE LORD TAKES AWAY.

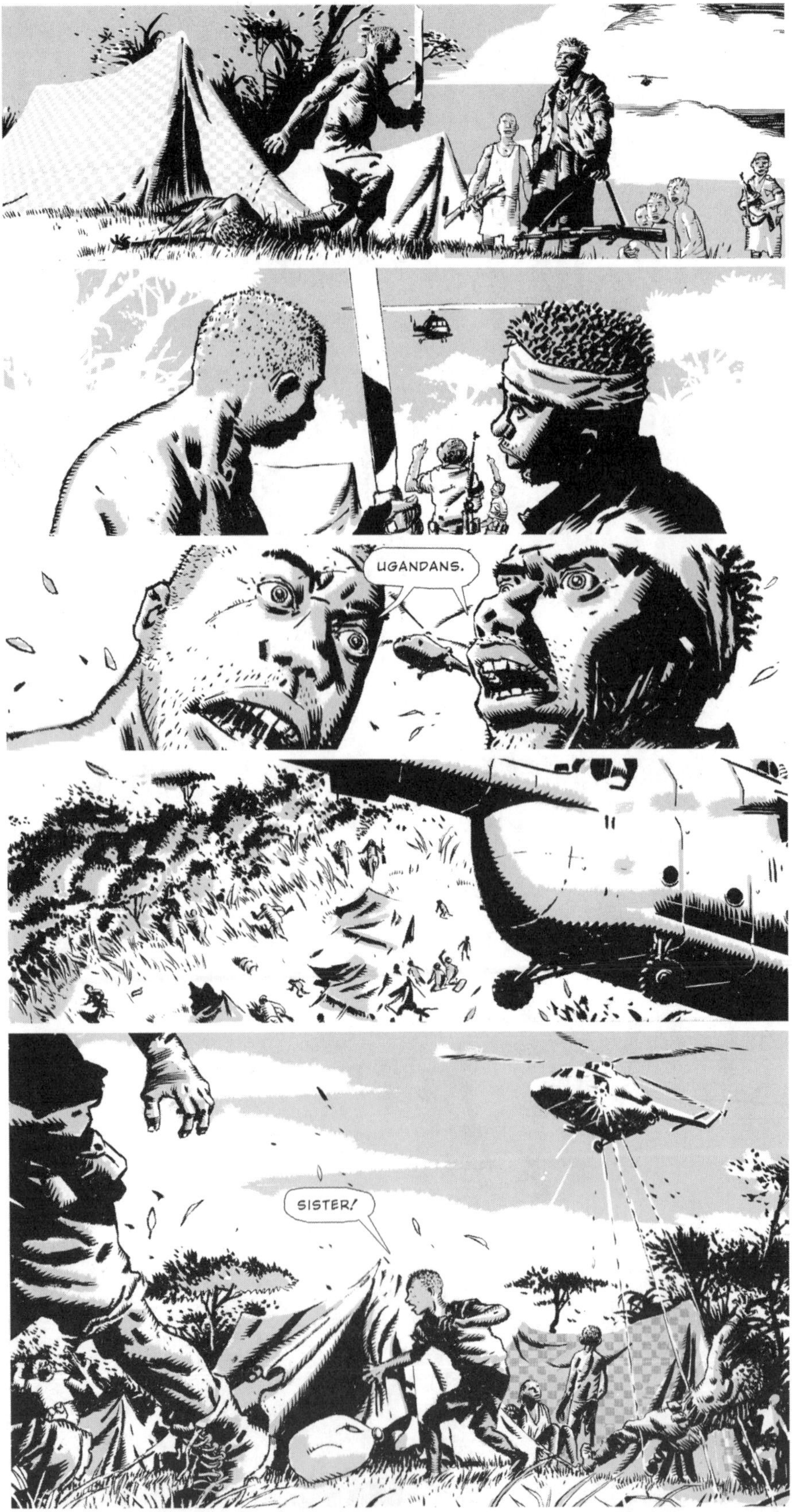
UGANDANS.
SISTER!

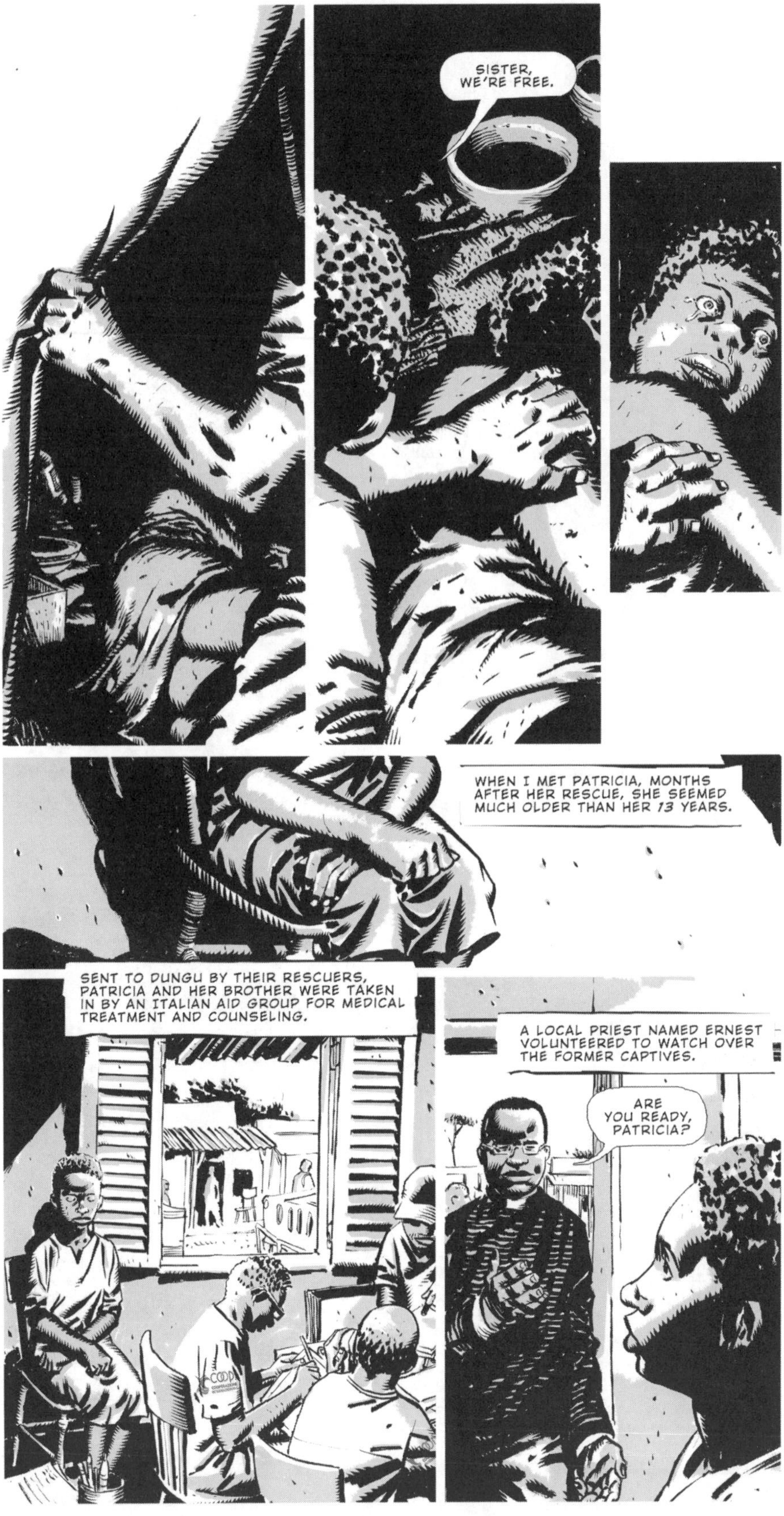

SISTER, WE'RE FREE.
WHEN I MET PATRICIA, MONTHS AFTER HER RESCUE, SHE SEEMED MUCH OLDER THAN HER 13 YEARS.
SENT TO DUNGU BY THEIR RESCUERS, PATRICIA AND HER BROTHER WERE TAKEN IN BY AN ITALIAN AID GROUP FOR MEDICAL TREATMENT AND COUNSELING.
A LOCAL PRIEST NAMED ERNEST VOLUNTEERED TO WATCH OVER THE FORMER CAPTIVES.
ARE YOU READY, PATRICIA?

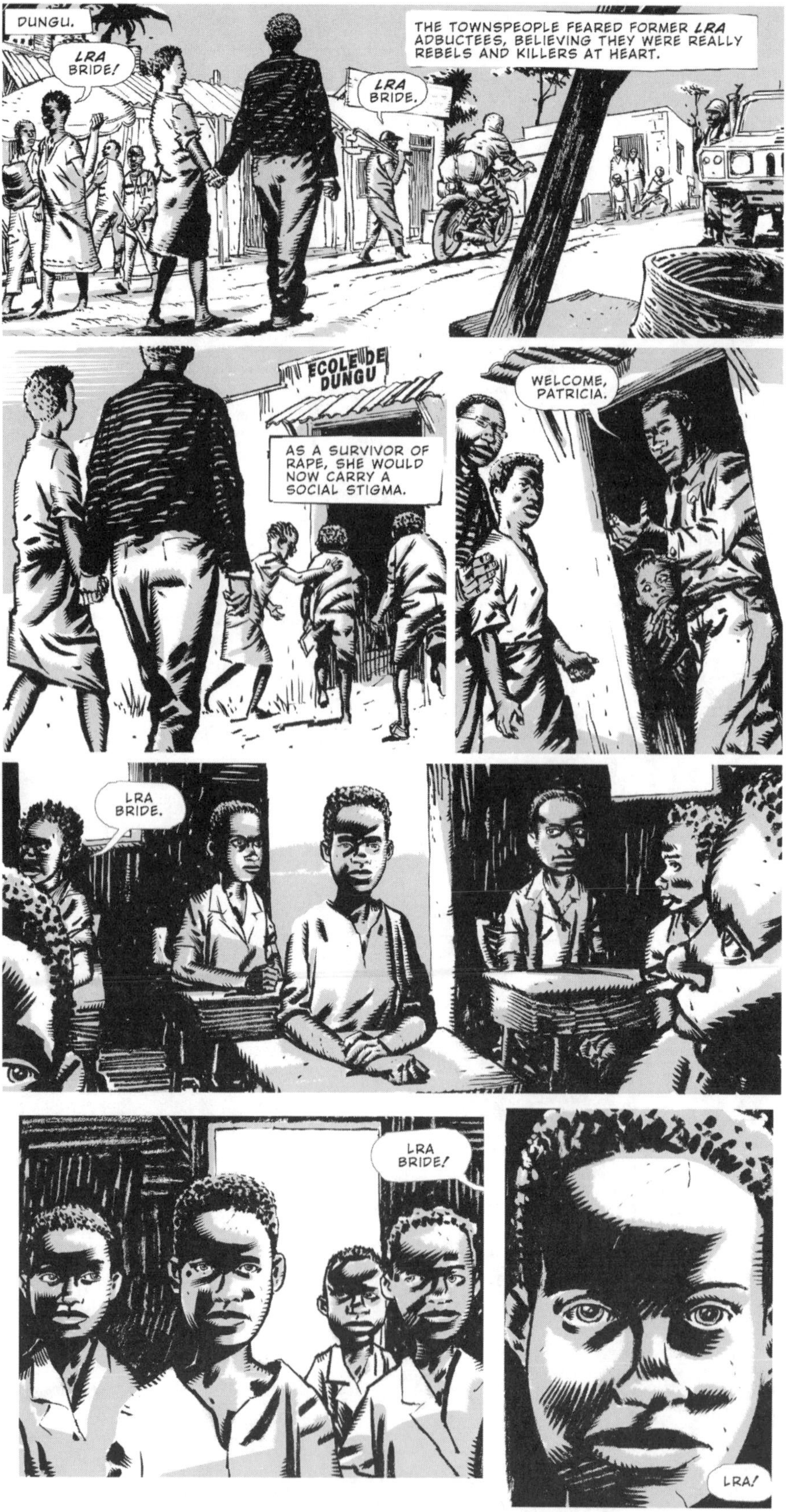
DUNGU.
LRA BRIDE!
LRA BRIDE.
THE TOWNSPEOPLE FEARED FORMER LRA ADBUCTEES, BELIEVING THEY WERE REALLY REBELS AND KILLERS AT HEART.
ECOLE DE DUNGU
AS A SURVIVOR OF RAPE, SHE WOULD NOW CARRY A SOCIAL STIGMA.
WELCOME, PATRICIA.
LRA BRIDE.
LRA BRIDE!
LRA!

CHAPTER SIX: HILLARY CLINTON

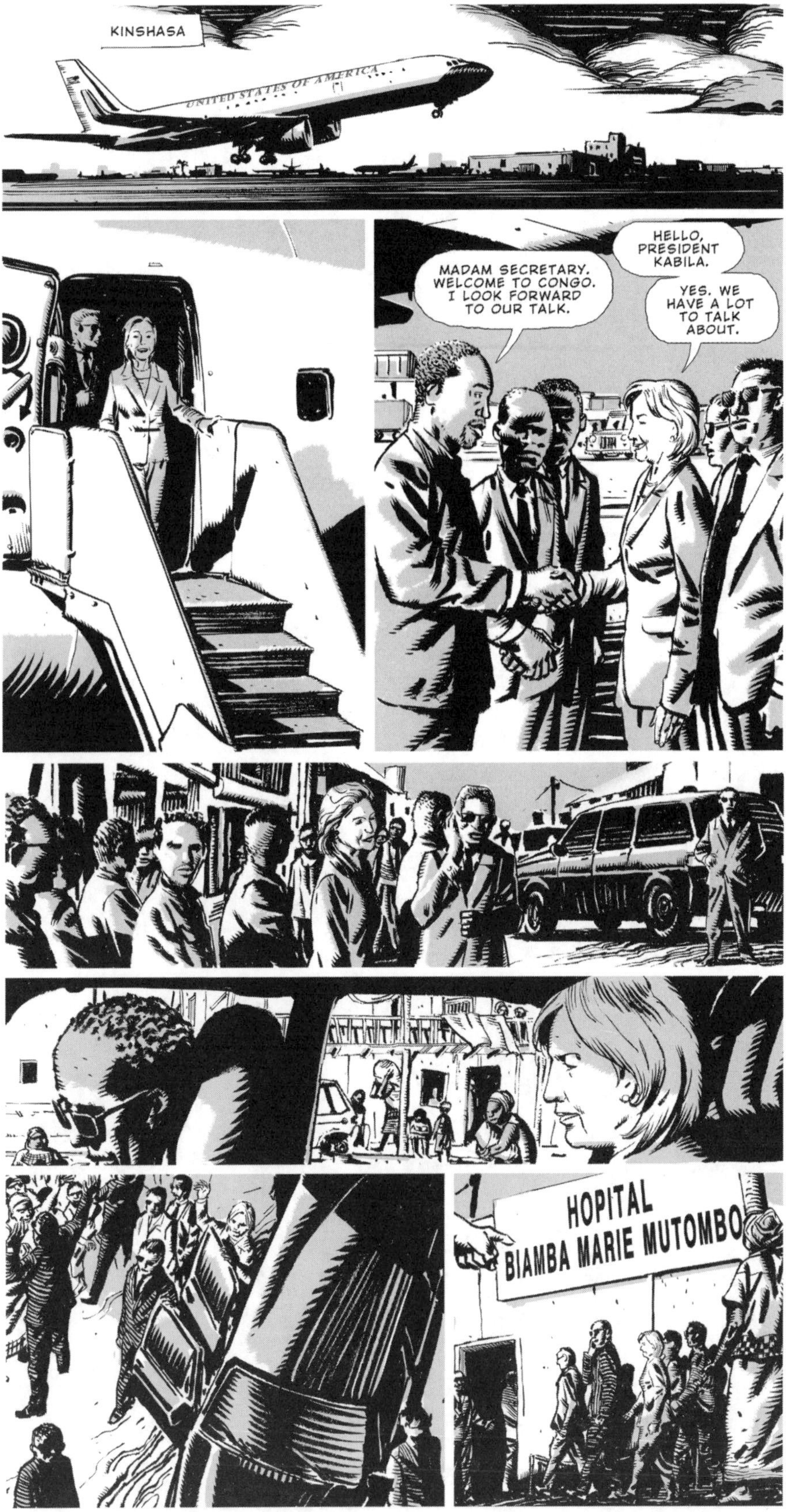
KINSHASA
UNITED STATES OF AMERICA
MADAM SECRETARY. WELCOME TO CONGO. I LOOK FORWARD TO OUR TALK.
HELLO, PRESIDENT KABILA.
YES. WE HAVE A LOT TO TALK ABOUT.
HOPITAL BIAMBA MARIE MUTOMBO

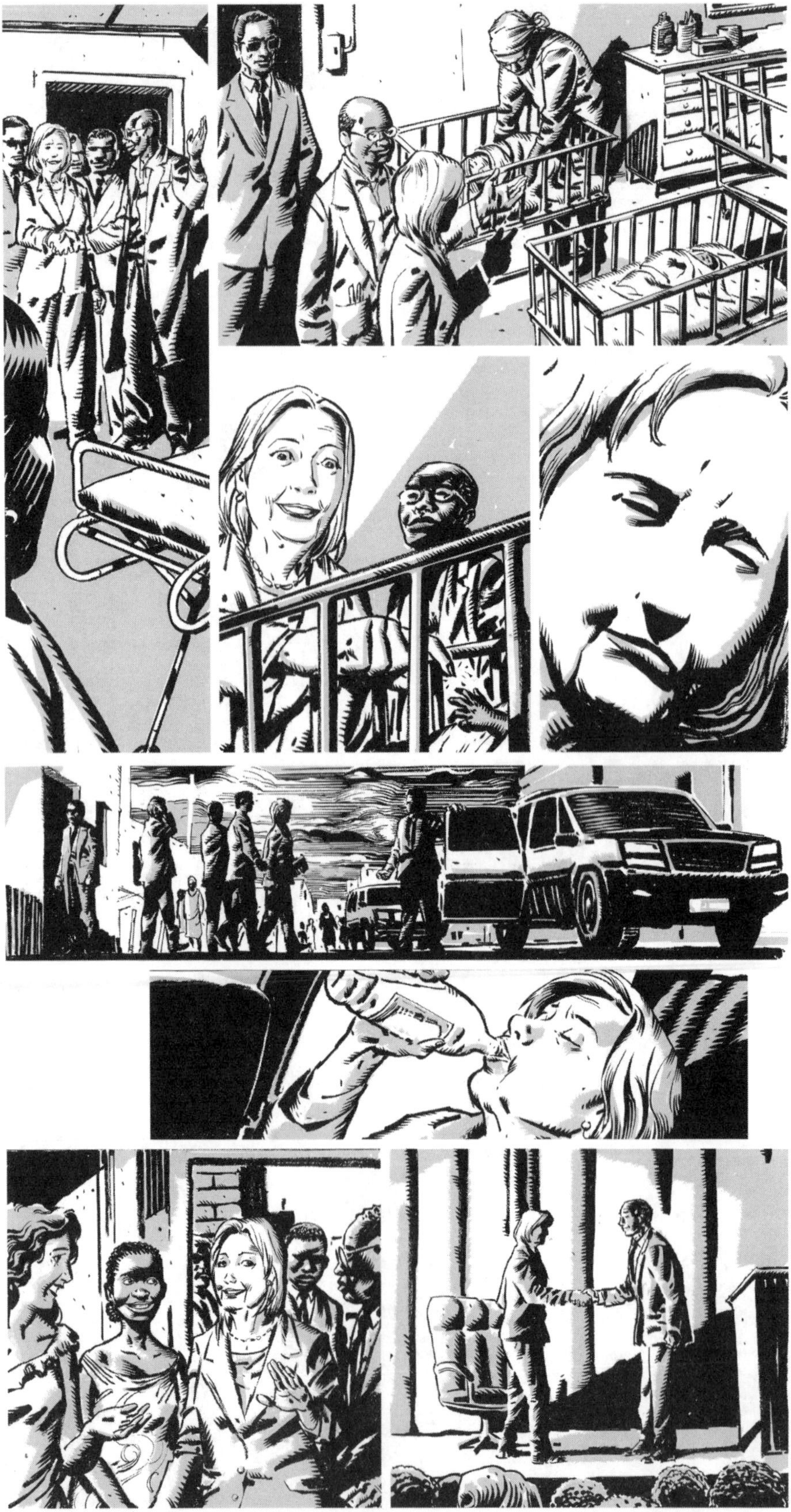

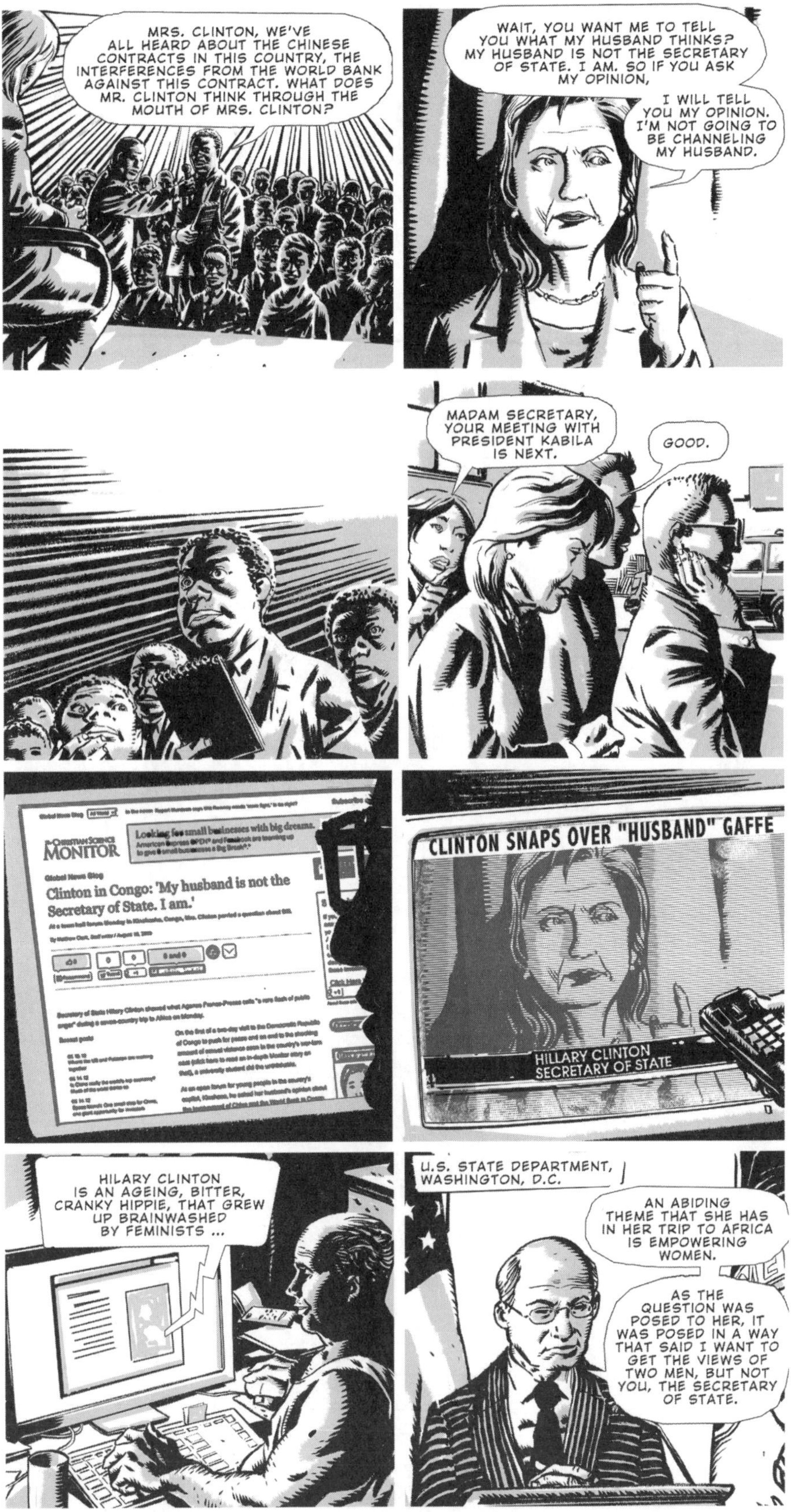
MRS. CLINTON, WE'VE ALL HEARD ABOUT THE CHINESE CONTRACTS IN THIS COUNTRY, THE INTERFERENCES FROM THE WORLD BANK AGAINST THIS CONTRACT. WHAT DOES MR. CLINTON THINK THROUGH THE MOUTH OF MRS. CLINTON?
WAIT, YOU WANT ME TO TELL YOU WHAT MY HUSBAND THINKS? MY HUSBAND IS NOT THE SECRETARY OF STATE. I AM. SO IF YOU ASK MY OPINION,
I WILL TELL YOU MY OPINION. I'M NOT GOING TO BE CHANNELING MY HUSBAND.
MADAM SECRETARY, YOUR MEETING WITH PRESIDENT KABILA IS NEXT.
GOOD.
MONITOR
Looking for small businesses with big dreams.
Global News Blog
Clinton in Congo: 'My husband is not the Secretary of State. I am.'
CLINTON SNAPS OVER "HUSBAND" GAFFE
HILLARY CLINTON
SECRETARY OF STATE
HILARY CLINTON IS AN AGEING, BITTER, CRANKY HIPPIE, THAT GREW UP BRAINWASHED BY FEMINISTS ...
U.S. STATE DEPARTMENT, WASHINGTON, D.C.
AN ABIDING THEME THAT SHE HAS IN HER TRIP TO AFRICA IS EMPOWERING WOMEN.
AS THE QUESTION WAS POSED TO HER, IT WAS POSED IN A WAY THAT SAID I WANT TO GET THE VIEWS OF TWO MEN, BUT NOT YOU, THE SECRETARY OF STATE.

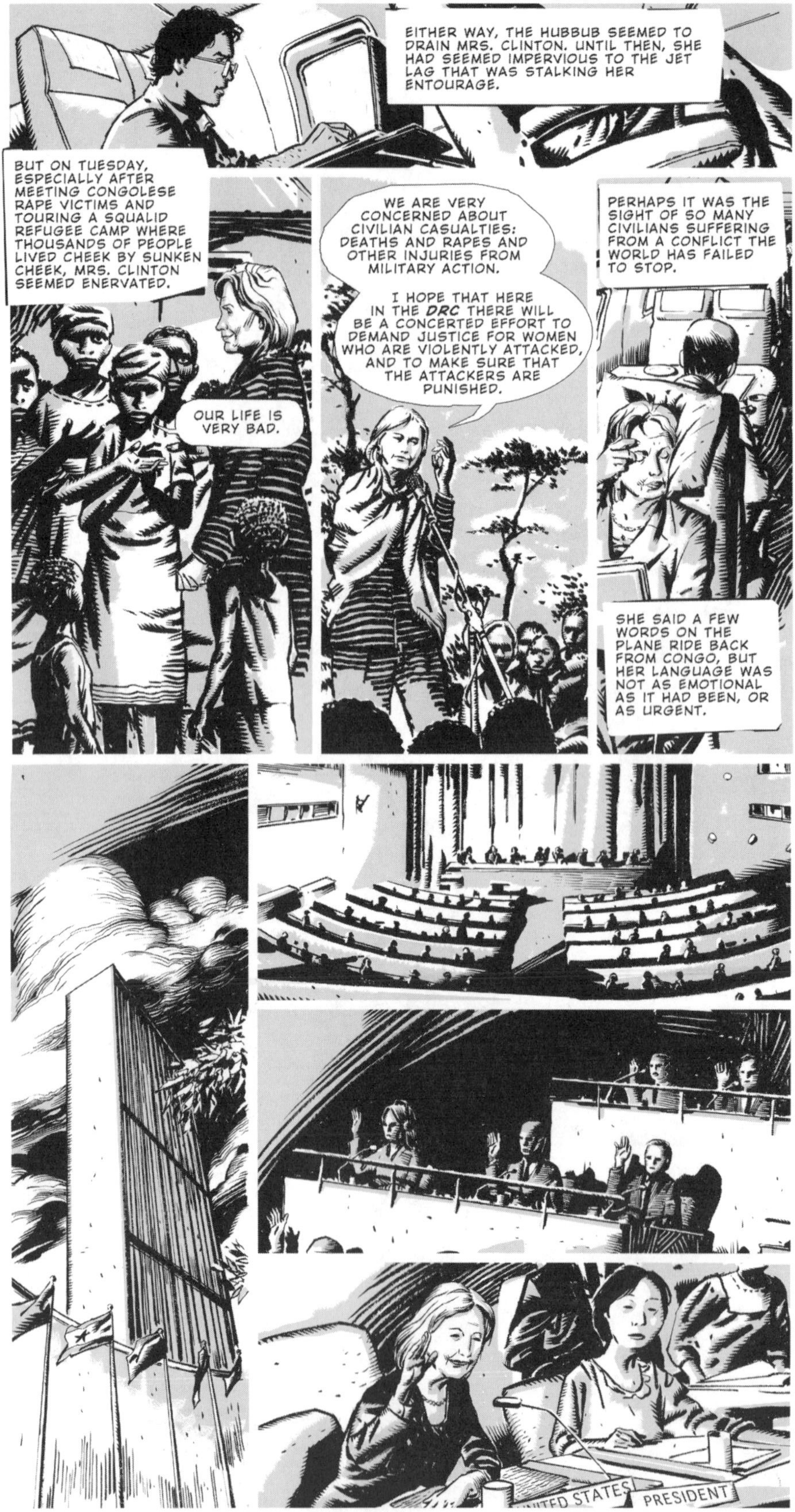
EITHER WAY, THE HUBBUB SEEMED TO DRAIN MRS. CLINTON. UNTIL THEN, SHE HAD SEEMED IMPERVIOUS TO THE JET LAG THAT WAS STALKING HER ENTOURAGE.
BUT ON TUESDAY, ESPECIALLY AFTER MEETING CONGOLESE RAPE VICTIMS AND TOURING A SQUALID REFUGEE CAMP WHERE THOUSANDS OF PEOPLE LIVED CHEEK BY SUNKEN CHEEK, MRS. CLINTON SEEMED ENERVATED.
OUR LIFE IS VERY BAD.
WE ARE VERY CONCERNED ABOUT CIVILIAN CASUALTIES: DEATHS AND RAPES AND OTHER INJURIES FROM MILITARY ACTION.
I HOPE THAT HERE IN THE DRC THERE WILL BE A CONCERTED EFFORT TO DEMAND JUSTICE FOR WOMEN WHO ARE VIOLENTLY ATTACKED, AND TO MAKE SURE THAT THE ATTACKERS ARE PUNISHED.
PERHAPS IT WAS THE SIGHT OF SO MANY CIVILIANS SUFFERING FROM A CONFLICT THE WORLD HAS FAILED TO STOP.
SHE SAID A FEW WORDS ON THE PLANE RIDE BACK FROM CONGO, BUT HER LANGUAGE WAS NOT AS EMOTIONAL AS IT HAD BEEN, OR AS URGENT.
PRESIDENT

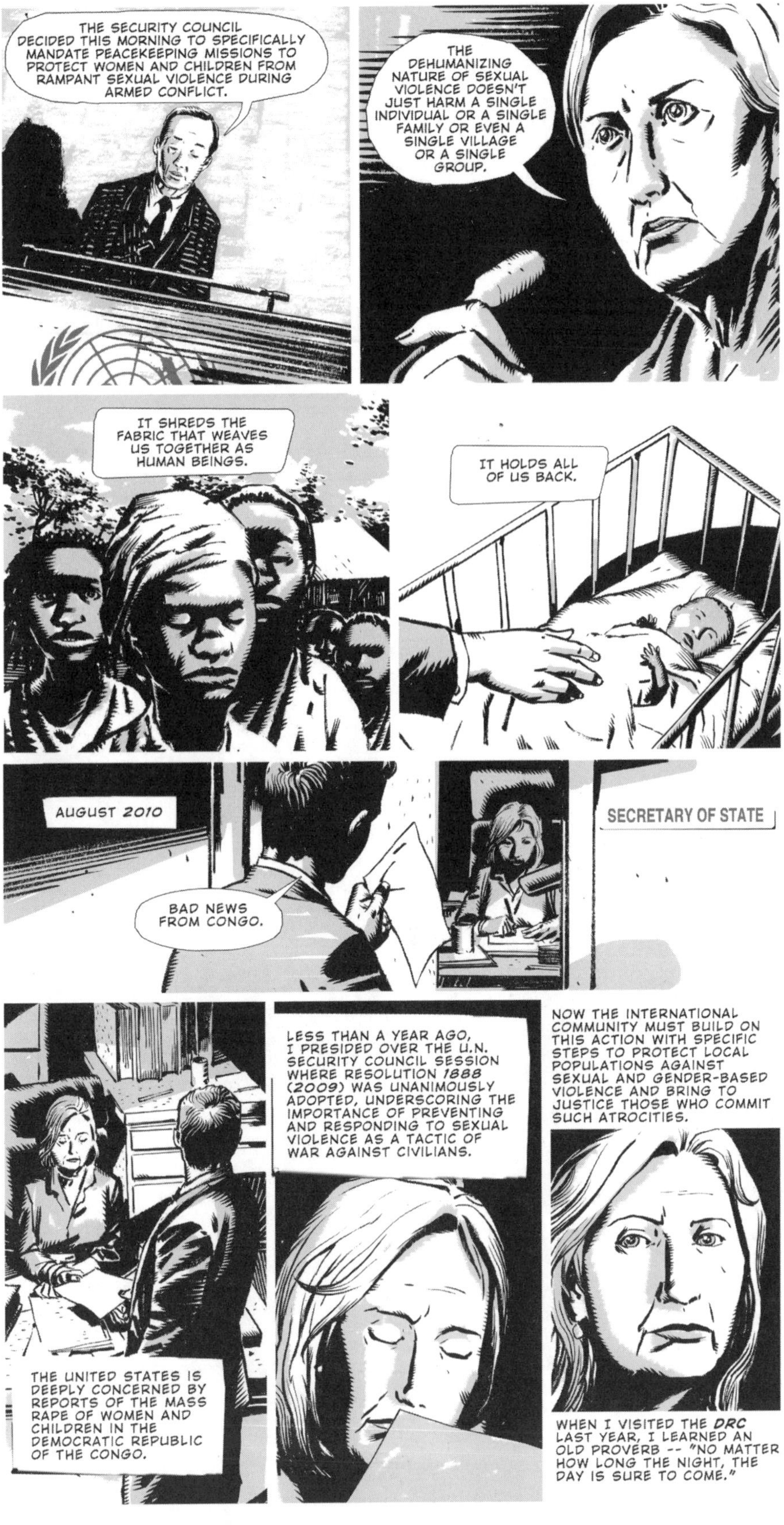

THE SECURITY COUNCIL DECIDED THIS MORNING TO SPECIFICALLY MANDATE PEACEKEEPING MISSIONS TO PROTECT WOMEN AND CHILDREN FROM RAMPANT SEXUAL VIOLENCE DURING ARMED CONFLICT.
THE DEHUMANIZING NATURE OF SEXUAL VIOLENCE DOESN'T JUST HARM A SINGLE INDIVIDUAL OR A SINGLE FAMILY OR EVEN A SINGLE VILLAGE OR A SINGLE GROUP.
IT SHREDS THE FABRIC THAT WEAVES US TOGETHER AS HUMAN BEINGS.
IT HOLDS ALL OF US BACK.
AUGUST 2010
SECRETARY OF STATE
BAD NEWS FROM CONGO.
THE UNITED STATES IS DEEPLY CONCERNED BY REPORTS OF THE MASS RAPE OF WOMEN AND CHILDREN IN THE DEMOCRATIC REPUBLIC OF THE CONGO.
LESS THAN A YEAR AGO, I PRESIDED OVER THE U.N. SECURITY COUNCIL SESSION WHERE RESOLUTION 1888 (2009) WAS UNANIMOUSLY ADOPTED, UNDERSCORING THE IMPORTANCE OF PREVENTING AND RESPONDING TO SEXUAL VIOLENCE AS A TACTIC OF WAR AGAINST CIVILIANS.
NOW THE INTERNATIONAL COMMUNITY MUST BUILD ON THIS ACTION WITH SPECIFIC STEPS TO PROTECT LOCAL POPULATIONS AGAINST SEXUAL AND GENDER-BASED VIOLENCE AND BRING TO JUSTICE THOSE WHO COMMIT SUCH ATROCITIES.
WHEN I VISITED THE DRC LAST YEAR, I LEARNED AN OLD PROVERB -- "NO MATTER HOW LONG THE NIGHT, THE DAY IS SURE TO COME."

CHAPTER SEVEN: THE PEACEKEEPERS

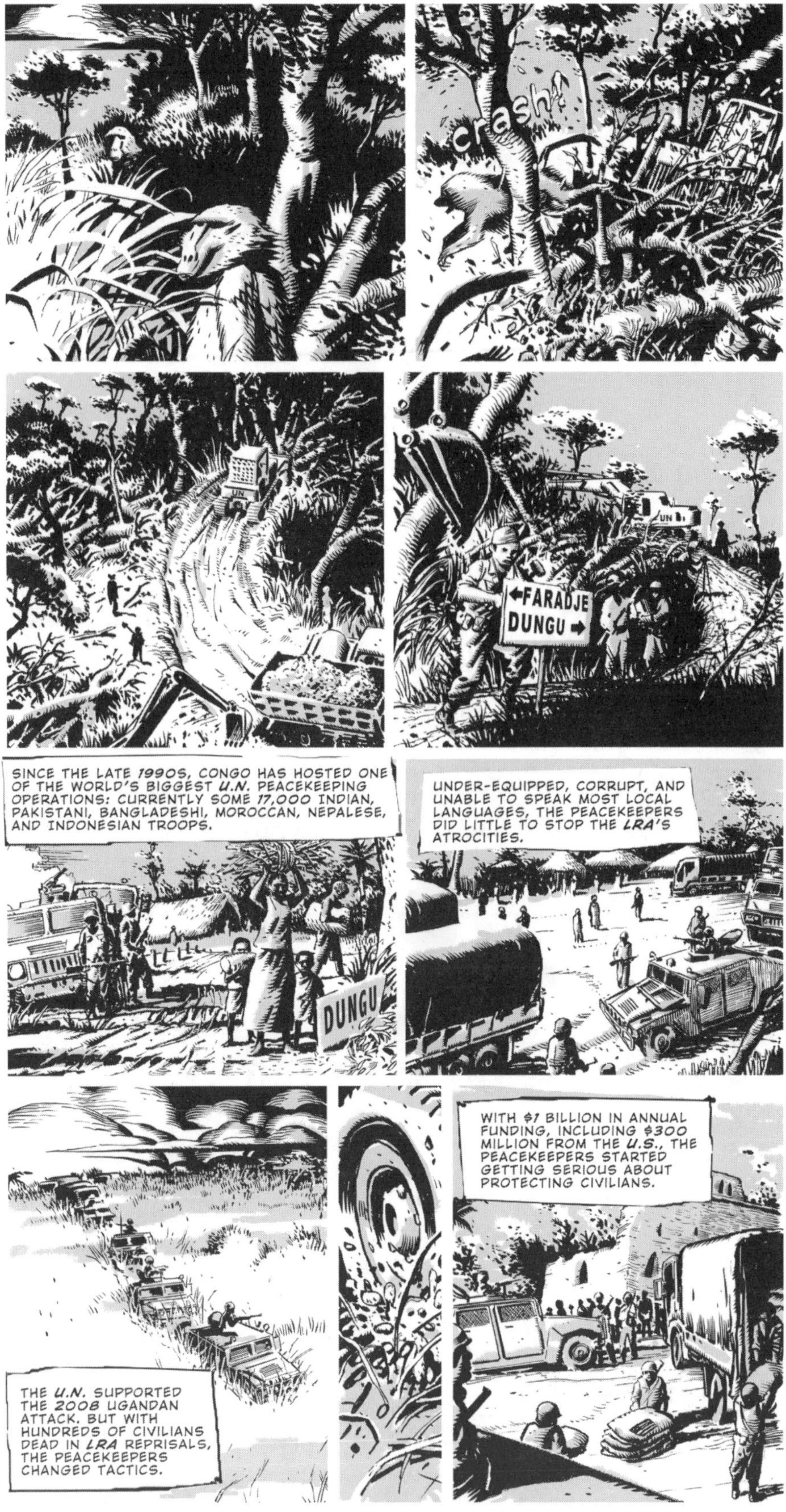

crash!!
FARADJE
DUNGU
SINCE THE LATE 1990S, CONGO HAS HOSTED ONE OF THE WORLD'S BIGGEST U.N. PEACEKEEPING OPERATIONS: CURRENTLY SOME 17,000 INDIAN, PAKISTANI, BANGLADESHI, MOROCCAN, NEPALESE, AND INDONESIAN TROOPS.
DUNGU
UNDER-EQUIPPED, CORRUPT, AND UNABLE TO SPEAK MOST LOCAL LANGUAGES, THE PEACEKEEPERS DID LITTLE TO STOP THE LRA'S ATROCITIES.
THE U.N. SUPPORTED THE 2008 UGANDAN ATTACK. BUT WITH HUNDREDS OF CIVILIANS DEAD IN LRA REPRISALS, THE PEACEKEEPERS CHANGED TACTICS.
WITH $1 BILLION IN ANNUAL FUNDING, INCLUDING $300 MILLION FROM THE U.S., THE PEACEKEEPERS STARTED GETTING SERIOUS ABOUT PROTECTING CIVILIANS.

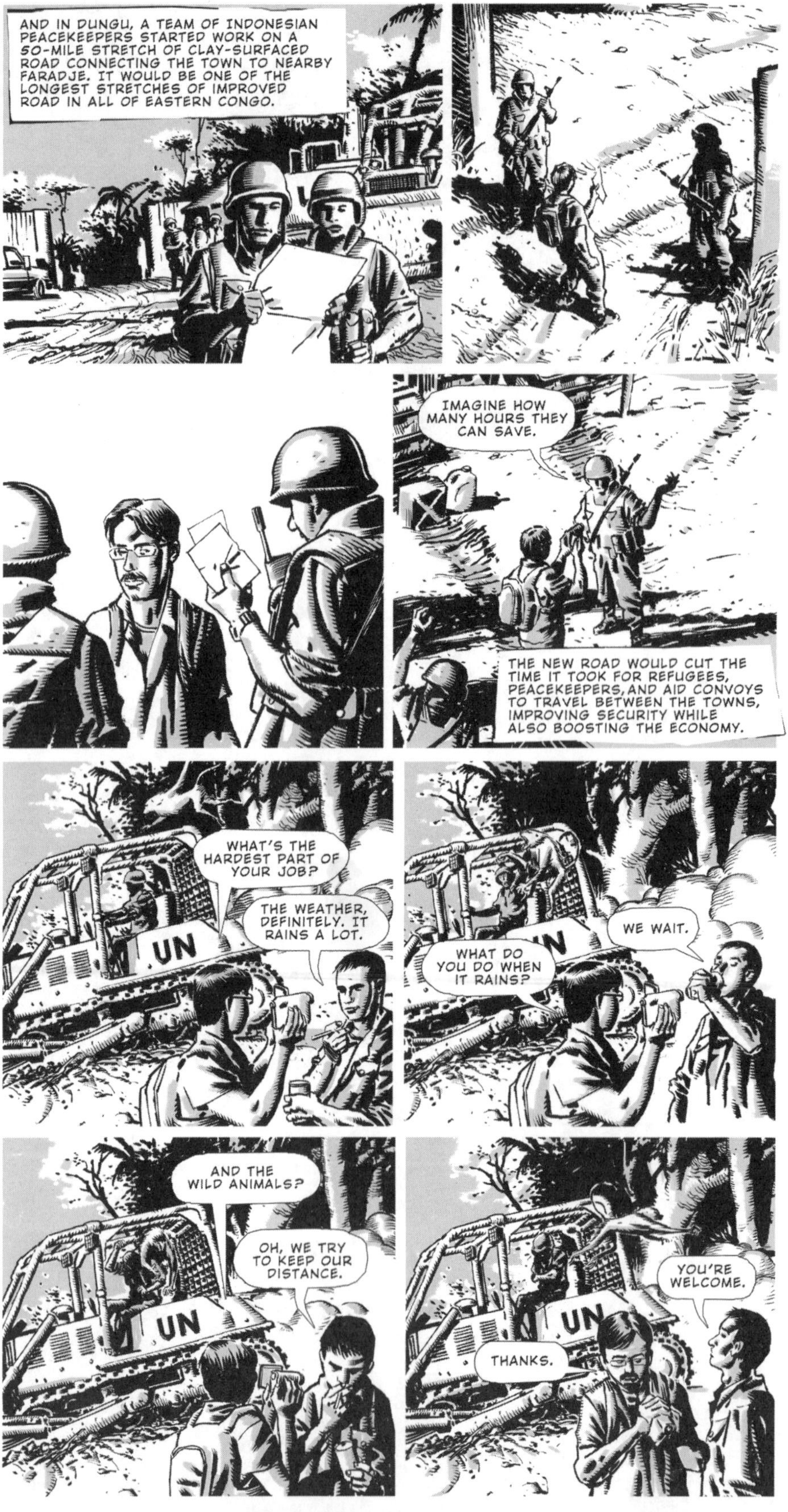
AND IN DUNGU, A TEAM OF INDONESIAN PEACEKEEPERS STARTED WORK ON A 50-MILE STRETCH OF CLAY-SURFACED ROAD CONNECTING THE TOWN TO NEARBY FARADJE. IT WOULD BE ONE OF THE LONGEST STRETCHES OF IMPROVED ROAD IN ALL OF EASTERN CONGO.
IMAGINE HOW MANY HOURS THEY CAN SAVE.
THE NEW ROAD WOULD CUT THE TIME IT TOOK FOR REFUGEES, PEACEKEEPERS, AND AID CONVOYS TO TRAVEL BETWEEN THE TOWNS, IMPROVING SECURITY WHILE ALSO BOOSTING THE ECONOMY.
WHAT'S THE HARDEST PART OF YOUR JOB?
THE WEATHER, DEFINITELY. IT RAINS A LOT.
UN
WHAT DO YOU DO WHEN IT RAINS?
WE WAIT.
AND THE WILD ANIMALS?
OH, WE TRY TO KEEP OUR DISTANCE.
UN
YOU'RE WELCOME.
THANKS.
UN

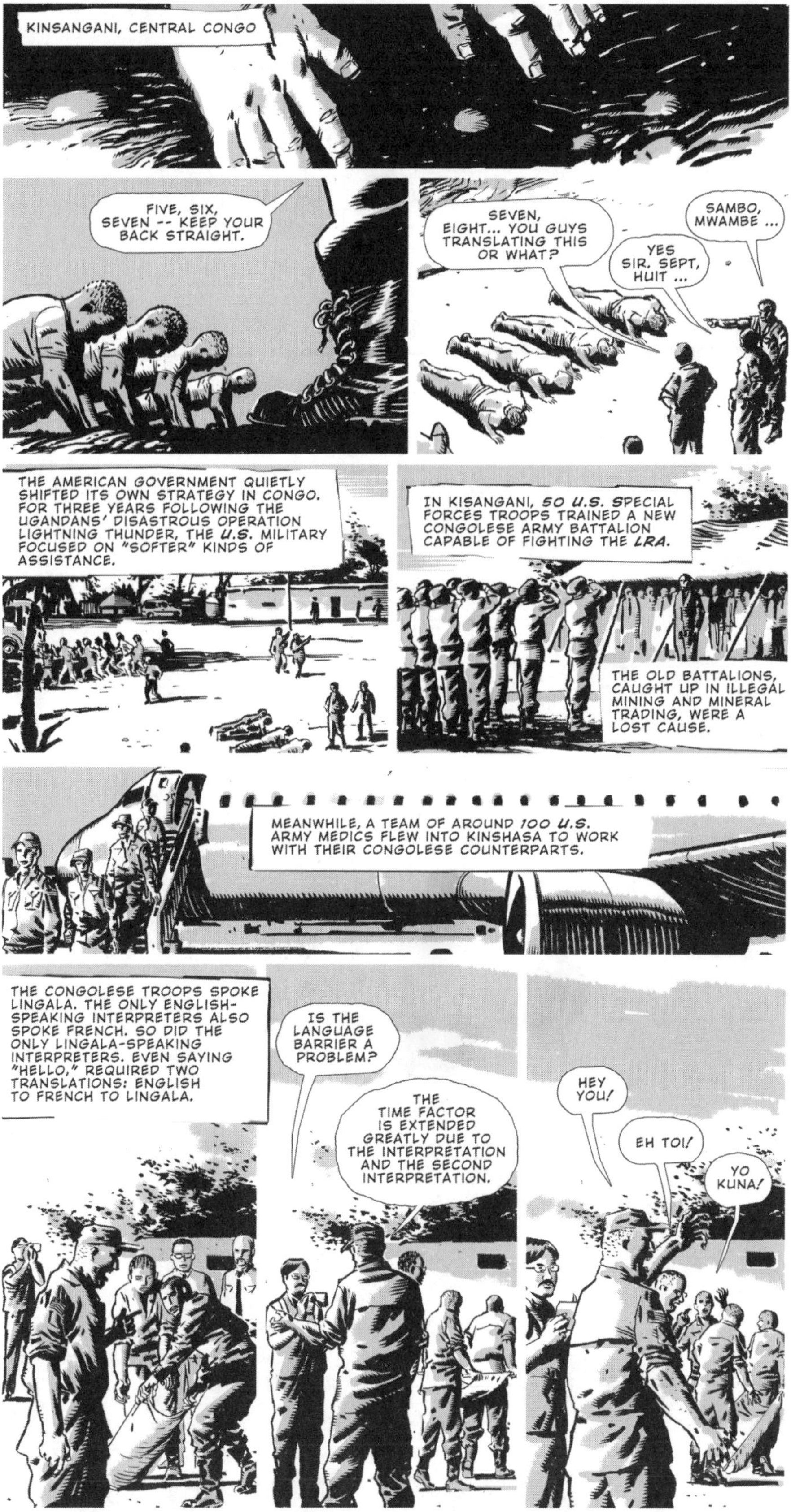
KINSANGANI, CENTRAL CONGO
FIVE, SIX, SEVEN -- KEEP YOUR BACK STRAIGHT.
SEVEN, EIGHT... YOU GUYS TRANSLATING THIS OR WHAT?
YES SIR. SEPT, HUIT ...
SAMBO, MWAMBE ...
THE AMERICAN GOVERNMENT QUIETLY SHIFTED ITS OWN STRATEGY IN CONGO. FOR THREE YEARS FOLLOWING THE UGANDANS' DISASTROUS OPERATION LIGHTNING THUNDER, THE U.S. MILITARY FOCUSED ON "SOFTER" KINDS OF ASSISTANCE.
IN KISANGANI, 50 U.S. SPECIAL FORCES TROOPS TRAINED A NEW CONGOLESE ARMY BATTALION CAPABLE OF FIGHTING THE LRA.
THE OLD BATTALIONS, CAUGHT UP IN ILLEGAL MINING AND MINERAL TRADING, WERE A LOST CAUSE.
MEANWHILE, A TEAM OF AROUND 100 U.S. ARMY MEDICS FLEW INTO KINSHASA TO WORK WITH THEIR CONGOLESE COUNTERPARTS.
THE CONGOLESE TROOPS SPOKE LINGALA. THE ONLY ENGLISH-SPEAKING INTERPRETERS ALSO SPOKE FRENCH. SO DID THE ONLY LINGALA-SPEAKING INTERPRETERS. EVEN SAYING "HELLO," REQUIRED TWO TRANSLATIONS: ENGLISH TO FRENCH TO LINGALA.
IS THE LANGUAGE BARRIER A PROBLEM?
THE TIME FACTOR IS EXTENDED GREATLY DUE TO THE INTERPRETATION AND THE SECOND INTERPRETATION.
HEY YOU!
EH TOI!
YO KUNA!

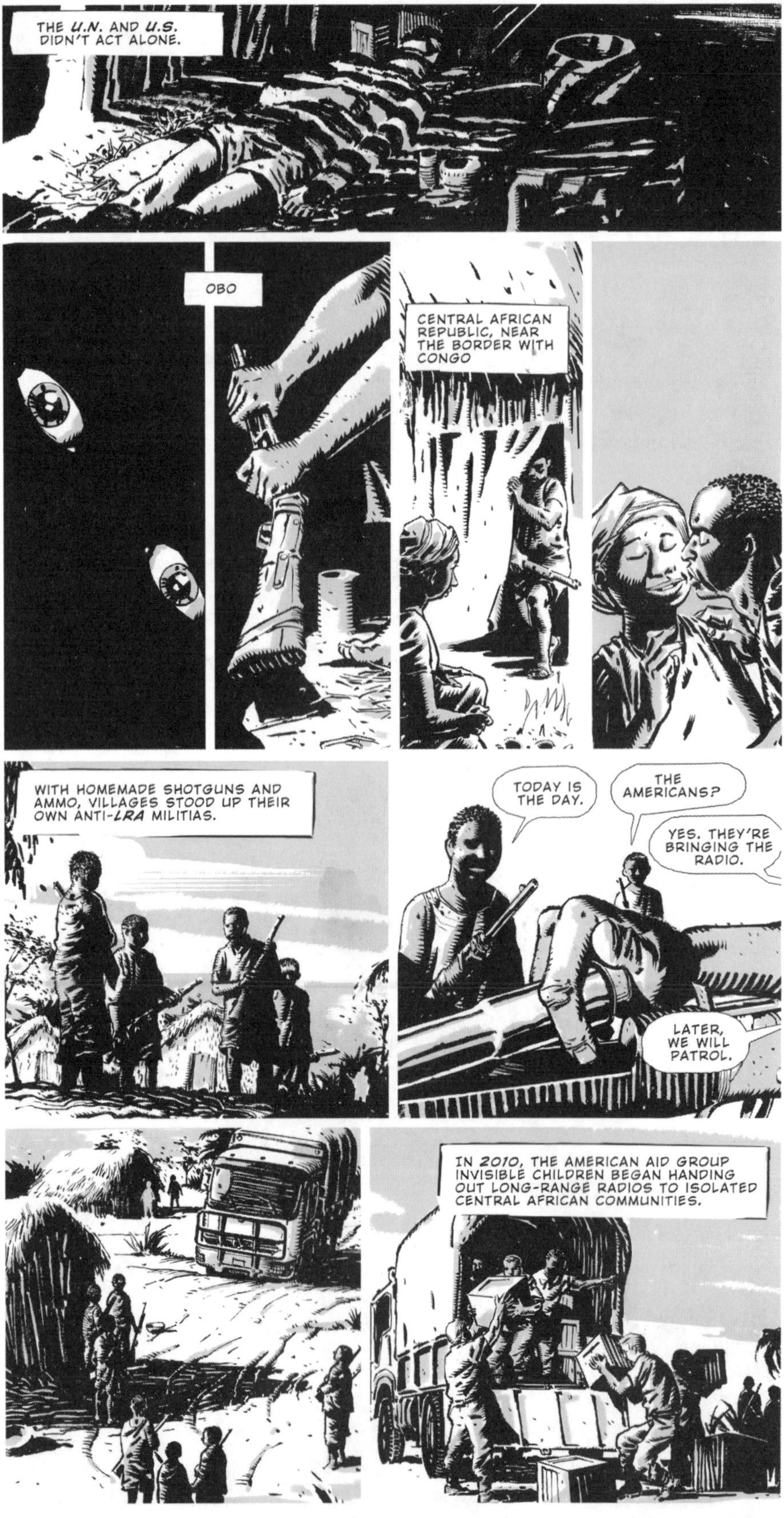
THE U.N. AND U.S. DIDN'T ACT ALONE.
OBO
CENTRAL AFRICAN REPUBLIC, NEAR THE BORDER WITH CONGO
WITH HOMEMADE SHOTGUNS AND AMMO, VILLAGES STOOD UP THEIR OWN ANTI-LRA MILITIAS.
TODAY IS THE DAY.
THE AMERICANS?
YES. THEY'RE BRINGING THE RADIO.
LATER, WE WILL PATROL.
IN 2010, THE AMERICAN AID GROUP INVISIBLE CHILDREN BEGAN HANDING OUT LONG-RANGE RADIOS TO ISOLATED CENTRAL AFRICAN COMMUNITIES.

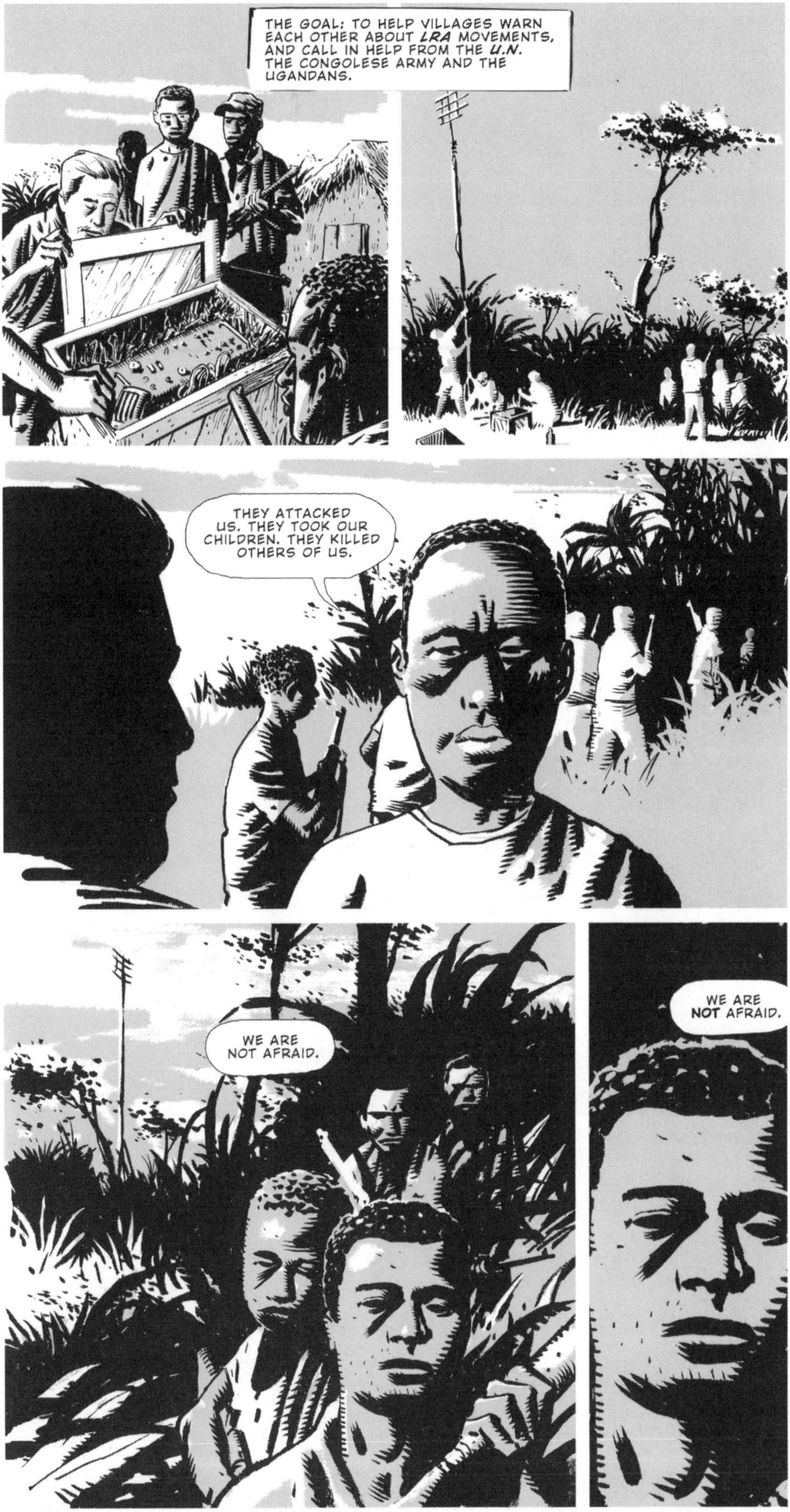
THE GOAL: TO HELP VILLAGES WARN EACH OTHER ABOUT *LRA* MOVEMENTS, AND CALL IN HELP FROM THE *U.N.* THE CONGOLESE ARMY AND THE UGANDANS.
THEY ATTACKED US. THEY TOOK OUR CHILDREN. THEY KILLED OTHERS OF US.
WE ARE NOT AFRAID.
WE ARE **NOT** AFRAID.

CHAPTER EIGHT: INVISIBLE CHILDREN

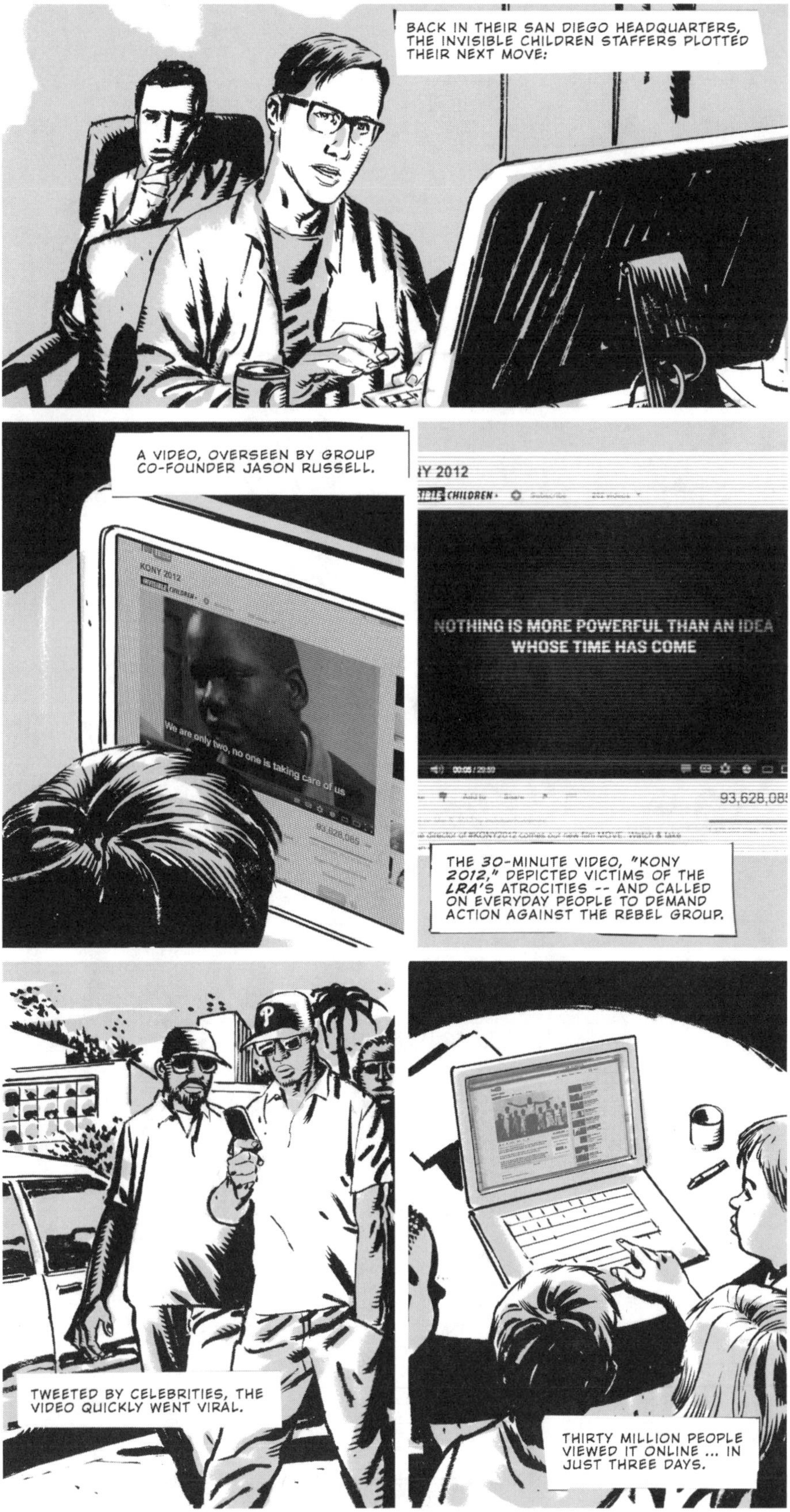
BACK IN THEIR SAN DIEGO HEADQUARTERS, THE INVISIBLE CHILDREN STAFFERS PLOTTED THEIR NEXT MOVE:
A VIDEO, OVERSEEN BY GROUP CO-FOUNDER JASON RUSSELL.
KONY 2012
We are only two, no one is taking care of us
NOTHING IS MORE POWERFUL THAN AN IDEA WHOSE TIME HAS COME
THE 30-MINUTE VIDEO, "KONY 2012," DEPICTED VICTIMS OF THE LRA'S ATROCITIES -- AND CALLED ON EVERYDAY PEOPLE TO DEMAND ACTION AGAINST THE REBEL GROUP.
TWEETED BY CELEBRITIES, THE VIDEO QUICKLY WENT VIRAL.
THIRTY MILLION PEOPLE VIEWED IT ONLINE ... IN JUST THREE DAYS.

CRITICS WERE MERCILESS TO INVISIBLE CHILDREN'S PROJECT.

IT HINTS UNCOMFORTABLY OF THE WHITE MAN'S BURDEN. THE SAVIOR ATTITUDE IS PERVASIVE IN ADVOCACY.

A PHOTO BY *AP* PHOTOGRAPHER GLENNA GORDON SURFACED, SHOWING RUSSELL AND HIS INVISIBLE *CHILDREN* CO-FOUNDERS LAREN POOLE AND BOBBY BAILEY GOOFING OFF WITH GUNS ON THE SUDAN-CONGO BORDER IN *2008*.

I FOUND ALL OF THEIR PREVIOUS EFFORTS TO BE EMOTIONALLY MANIPULATIVE, AND ALL THE THINGS I TRY AS A JOURNALIST NOT TO BE.

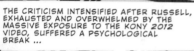

THE CRITICISM INTENSIFIED AFTER RUSSELL, EXHAUSTED AND OVERWHELMED BY THE MASSIVE EXPOSURE TO THE KONY *2012* VIDEO, SUFFERED A PSYCHOLOGICAL BREAK ...

...AND WAS FOUND NAKED AND RAVING ON A SAN DIEGO STREET CORNER.

RUSSELL SPENT MONTHS RECUPERATING BEFORE RETURNING TO WORK WITH INVISIBLE CHILDREN.

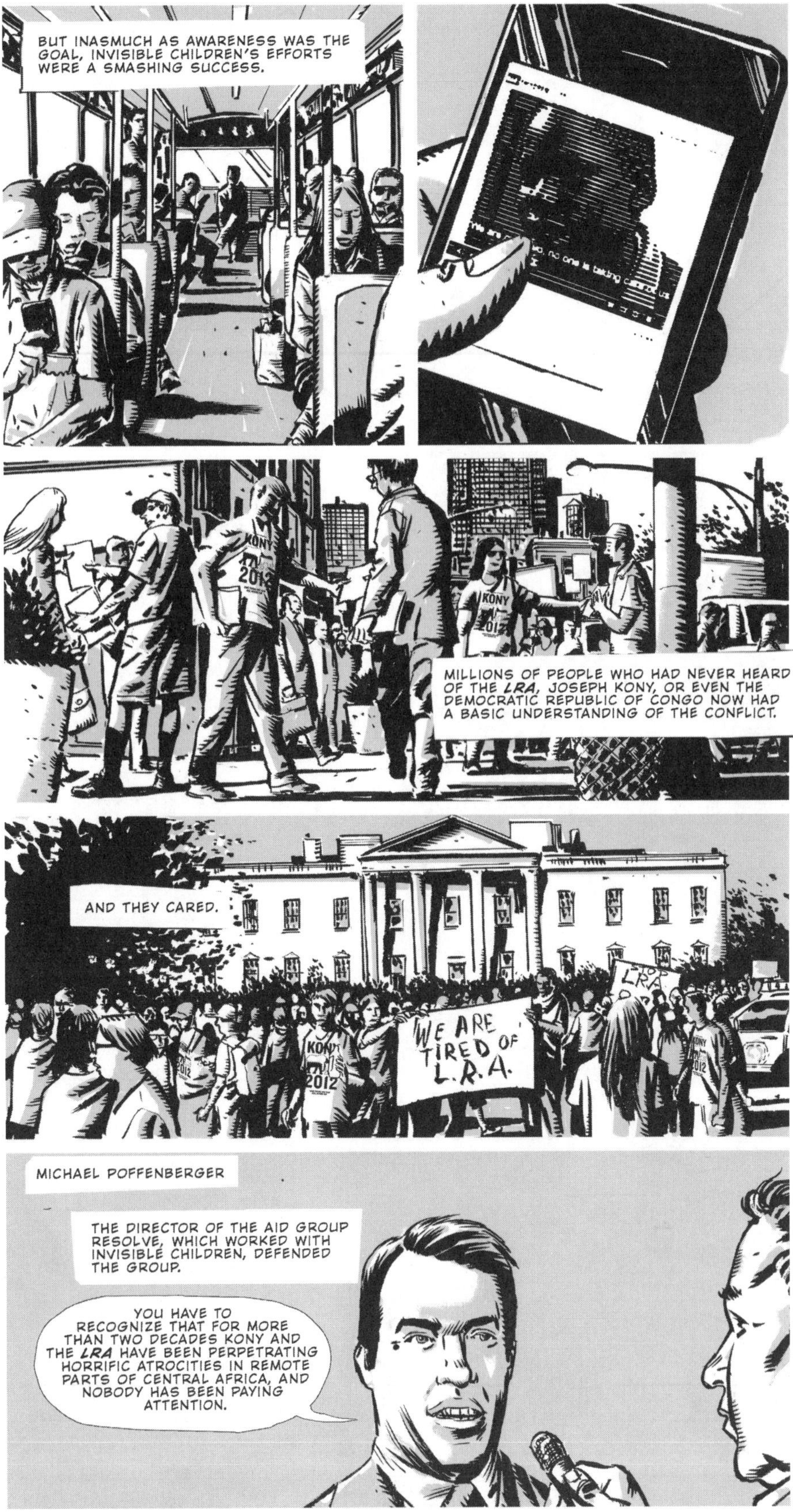
BUT INASMUCH AS AWARENESS WAS THE GOAL, INVISIBLE CHILDREN'S EFFORTS WERE A SMASHING SUCCESS.
KONY 2012
MILLIONS OF PEOPLE WHO HAD NEVER HEARD OF THE *LRA*, JOSEPH KONY, OR EVEN THE DEMOCRATIC REPUBLIC OF CONGO NOW HAD A BASIC UNDERSTANDING OF THE CONFLICT.
AND THEY CARED.
WE ARE TIRED OF L.R.A.
STOP LRA
MICHAEL POFFENBERGER
THE DIRECTOR OF THE AID GROUP RESOLVE, WHICH WORKED WITH INVISIBLE CHILDREN, DEFENDED THE GROUP.
YOU HAVE TO RECOGNIZE THAT FOR MORE THAN TWO DECADES KONY AND THE *LRA* HAVE BEEN PERPETRATING HORRIFIC ATROCITIES IN REMOTE PARTS OF CENTRAL AFRICA, AND NOBODY HAS BEEN PAYING ATTENTION.

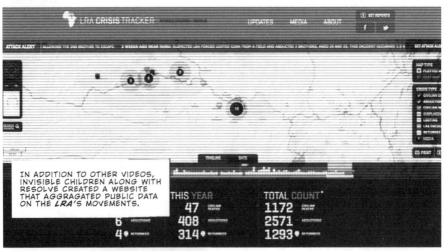

LRA CRISIS TRACKER
UPDATES
MEDIA
ABOUT
ATTACK ALERT
TIMELINE
DATE
IN ADDITION TO OTHER VIDEOS, INVISIBLE CHILDREN ALONG WITH RESOLVE CREATED A WEBSITE THAT AGGRAGATED PUBLIC DATA ON THE LRA'S MOVEMENTS.
THIS YEAR
TOTAL COUNT*
6
4
47
408
314
1172
2571
1293
THREE LRA FIGHTERS SPOTTED NEAR DUNGU!
THE LRA CRISIS TRACKER SUBJECTED THE REBEL GROUP TO UNPRECEDENTED PUBLIC EXPOSURE, IN NEAR REAL TIME.
Tambura
Mapoi
Obo
Ezo
Lingasi
Dorum
Khogbo
Li Rangu
Yambio
Diagbe
Sakure
Niangara
Dungu
ANYONE WITH INTERNET ACCESS COULD READ REPORTS OF LRA SIGHTING AND TRACK THE GROUP'S WINDING PATH ACROSS CENTRAL AFRICA -- ALTHOUGH NOT TERRIBLY ACCURATELY.
TRUE, BY THE TIME THE KONY 2012 VIDEO AND LRA CRISIS TRACKER HAD LAUNCHED, THE U.S. AND ITS ALLIES WERE ALREADY BUSILY HUNTING KONY IN CENTRAL AFRICA.
BUT THE POPULAR AWARENESS ENSURED THERE WAS A MEASURE OF ACCOUNTABILITY FOR THE MILITARY EFFORTS.
GUESS WHAT THE LRA DID TODAY.

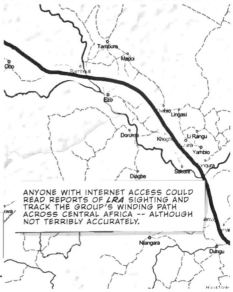

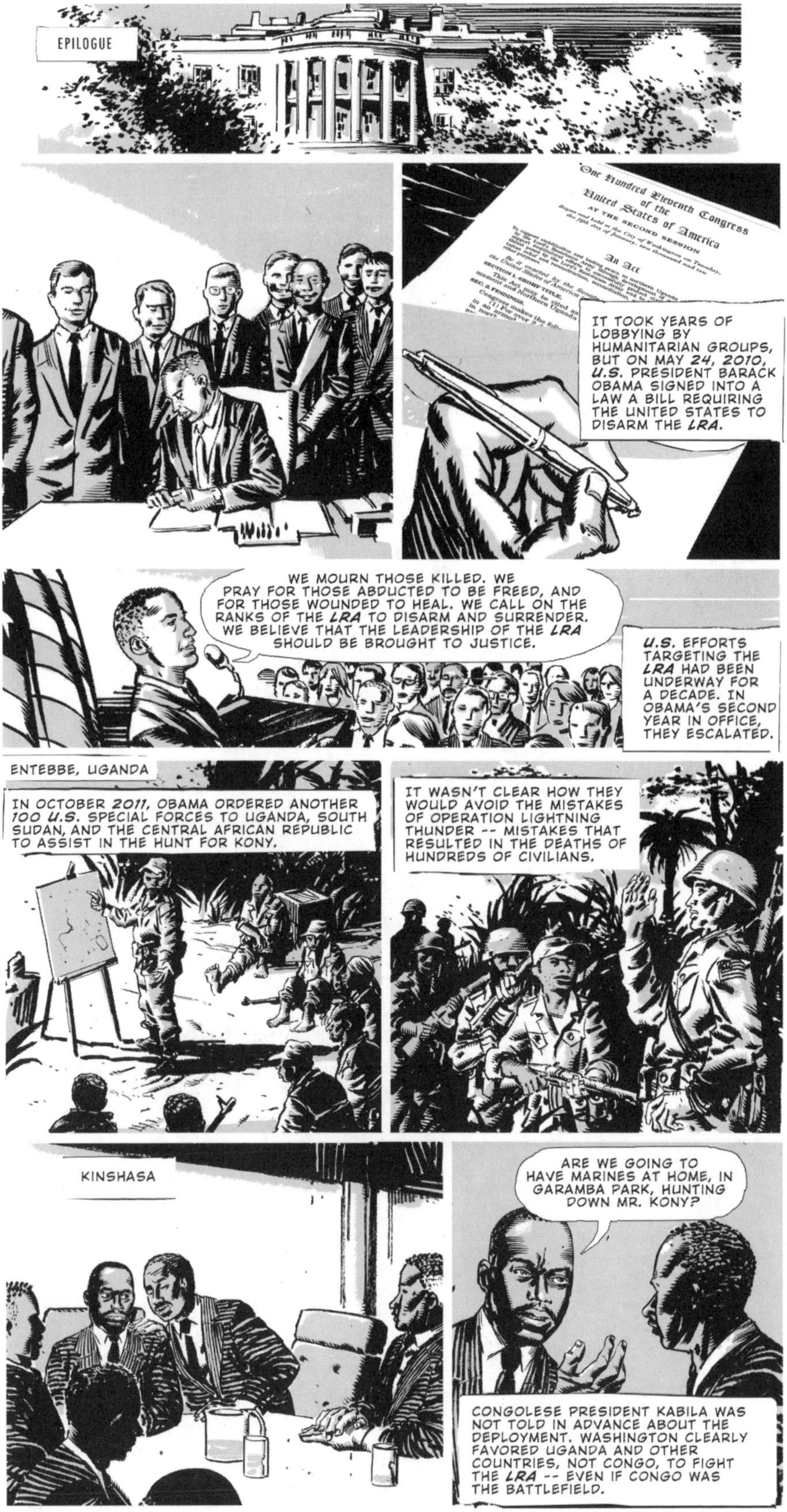
EPILOGUE
One Hundred Eleventh Congress
of the
United States of America
AT THE SECOND SESSION
An Act
IT TOOK YEARS OF LOBBYING BY HUMANITARIAN GROUPS, BUT ON MAY 24, 2010, U.S. PRESIDENT BARACK OBAMA SIGNED INTO A LAW A BILL REQUIRING THE UNITED STATES TO DISARM THE LRA.
WE MOURN THOSE KILLED. WE PRAY FOR THOSE ABDUCTED TO BE FREED, AND FOR THOSE WOUNDED TO HEAL. WE CALL ON THE RANKS OF THE LRA TO DISARM AND SURRENDER. WE BELIEVE THAT THE LEADERSHIP OF THE LRA SHOULD BE BROUGHT TO JUSTICE.
U.S. EFFORTS TARGETING THE LRA HAD BEEN UNDERWAY FOR A DECADE. IN OBAMA'S SECOND YEAR IN OFFICE, THEY ESCALATED.
ENTEBBE, UGANDA
IN OCTOBER 2011, OBAMA ORDERED ANOTHER 100 U.S. SPECIAL FORCES TO UGANDA, SOUTH SUDAN, AND THE CENTRAL AFRICAN REPUBLIC TO ASSIST IN THE HUNT FOR KONY.
IT WASN'T CLEAR HOW THEY WOULD AVOID THE MISTAKES OF OPERATION LIGHTNING THUNDER -- MISTAKES THAT RESULTED IN THE DEATHS OF HUNDREDS OF CIVILIANS.
KINSHASA
ARE WE GOING TO HAVE MARINES AT HOME, IN GARAMBA PARK, HUNTING DOWN MR. KONY?
CONGOLESE PRESIDENT KABILA WAS NOT TOLD IN ADVANCE ABOUT THE DEPLOYMENT. WASHINGTON CLEARLY FAVORED UGANDA AND OTHER COUNTRIES, NOT CONGO, TO FIGHT THE LRA -- EVEN IF CONGO WAS THE BATTLEFIELD.

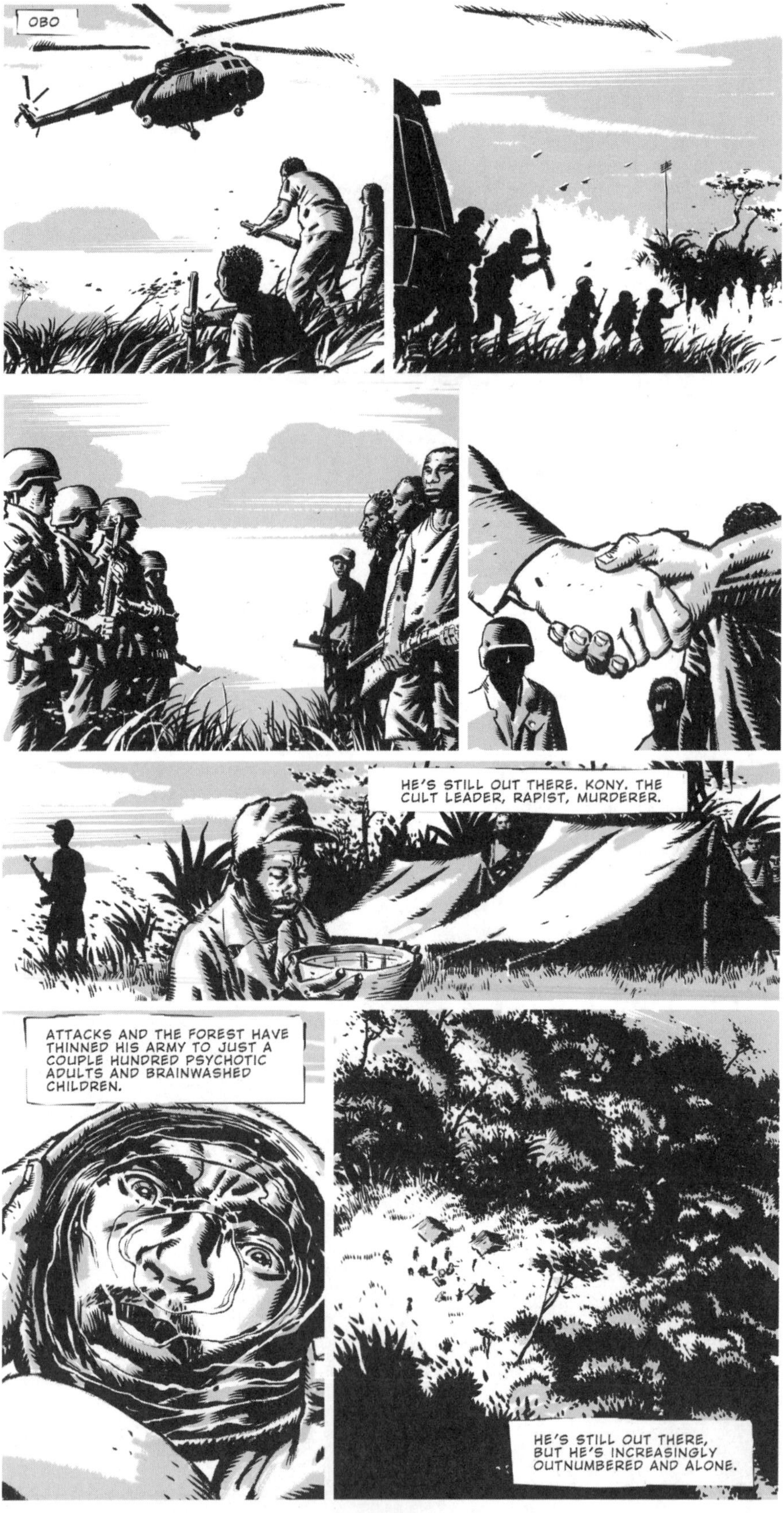
OBO
HE'S STILL OUT THERE. KONY. THE CULT LEADER, RAPIST, MURDERER.
ATTACKS AND THE FOREST HAVE THINNED HIS ARMY TO JUST A COUPLE HUNDRED PSYCHOTIC ADULTS AND BRAINWASHED CHILDREN.
HE'S STILL OUT THERE, BUT HE'S INCREASINGLY OUTNUMBERED AND ALONE.

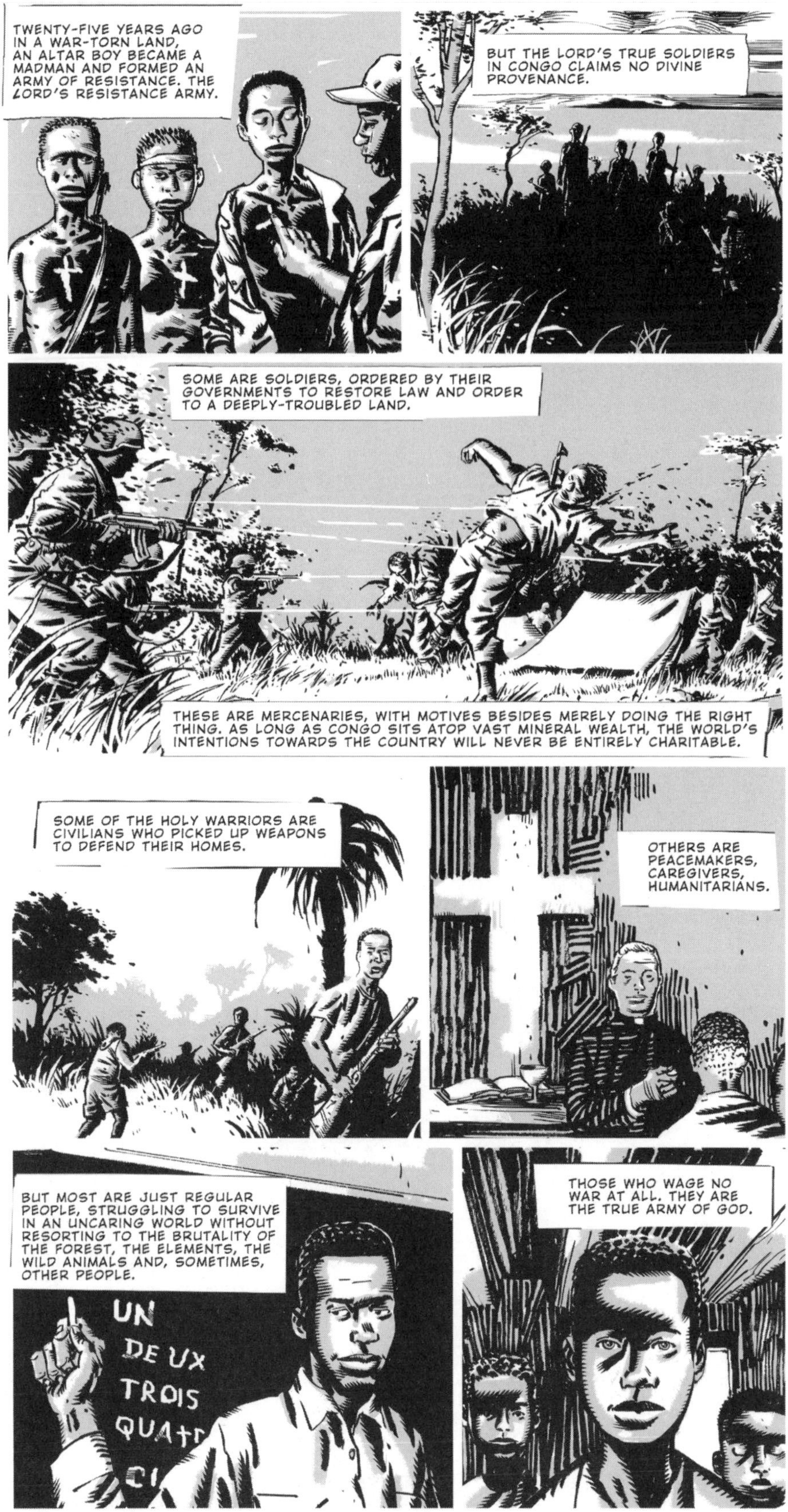
TWENTY-FIVE YEARS AGO IN A WAR-TORN LAND, AN ALTAR BOY BECAME A MADMAN AND FORMED AN ARMY OF RESISTANCE. THE LORD'S RESISTANCE ARMY.
BUT THE LORD'S TRUE SOLDIERS IN CONGO CLAIMS NO DIVINE PROVENANCE.
SOME ARE SOLDIERS, ORDERED BY THEIR GOVERNMENTS TO RESTORE LAW AND ORDER TO A DEEPLY-TROUBLED LAND.
THESE ARE MERCENARIES, WITH MOTIVES BESIDES MERELY DOING THE RIGHT THING. AS LONG AS CONGO SITS ATOP VAST MINERAL WEALTH, THE WORLD'S INTENTIONS TOWARDS THE COUNTRY WILL NEVER BE ENTIRELY CHARITABLE.
SOME OF THE HOLY WARRIORS ARE CIVILIANS WHO PICKED UP WEAPONS TO DEFEND THEIR HOMES.
OTHERS ARE PEACEMAKERS, CAREGIVERS, HUMANITARIANS.
BUT MOST ARE JUST REGULAR PEOPLE, STRUGGLING TO SURVIVE IN AN UNCARING WORLD WITHOUT RESORTING TO THE BRUTALITY OF THE FOREST, THE ELEMENTS, THE WILD ANIMALS AND, SOMETIMES, OTHER PEOPLE.
UN
DEUX
TROIS
THOSE WHO WAGE NO WAR AT ALL. THEY ARE THE TRUE ARMY OF GOD.

POSTSCRIPT: THE REBEL MAJOR GENERAL

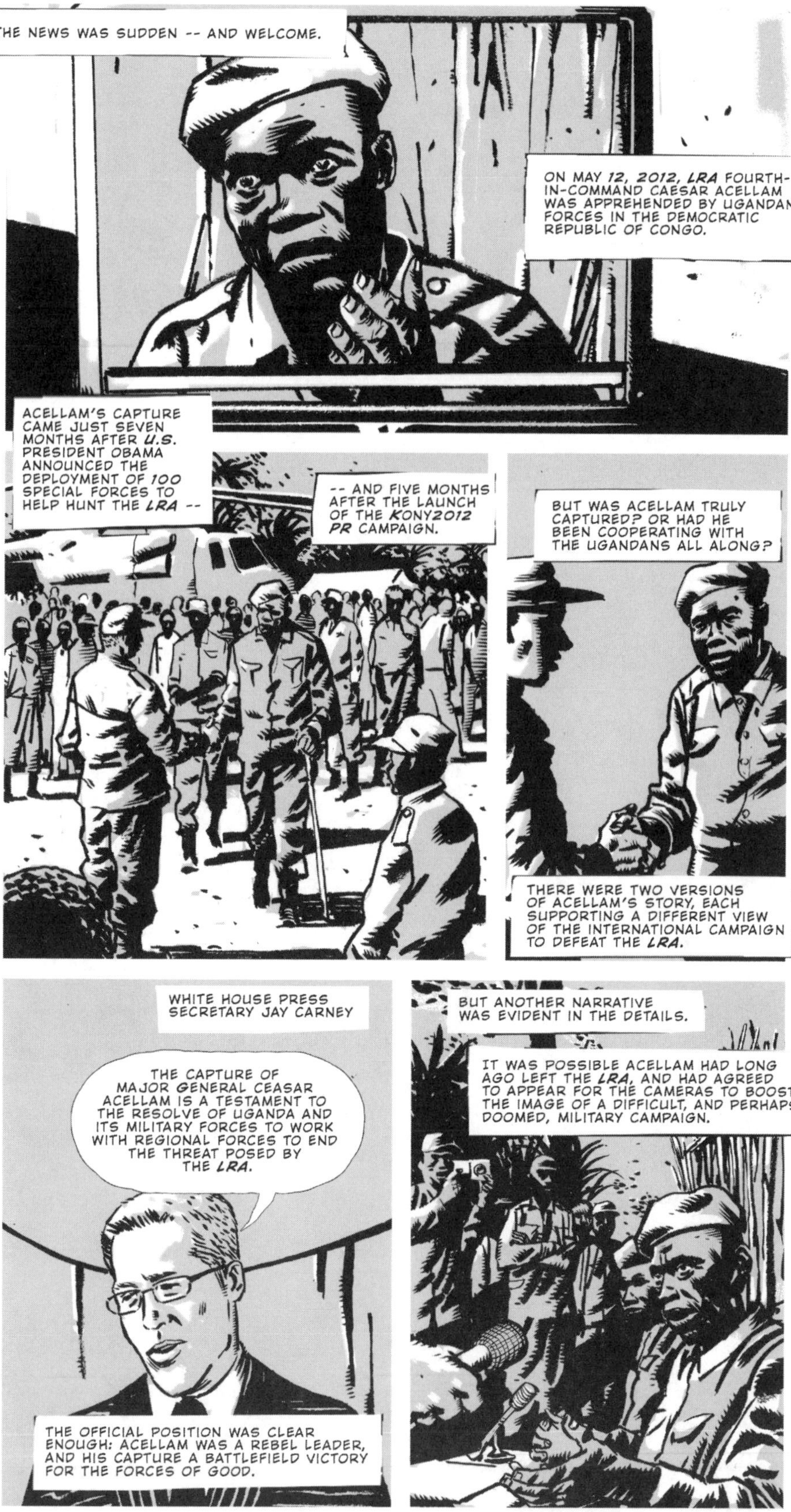
THE NEWS WAS SUDDEN -- AND WELCOME.
ON MAY 12, 2012, LRA FOURTH-IN-COMMAND CAESAR ACELLAM WAS APPREHENDED BY UGANDAN FORCES IN THE DEMOCRATIC REPUBLIC OF CONGO.
ACELLAM'S CAPTURE CAME JUST SEVEN MONTHS AFTER U.S. PRESIDENT OBAMA ANNOUNCED THE DEPLOYMENT OF 100 SPECIAL FORCES TO HELP HUNT THE LRA --
-- AND FIVE MONTHS AFTER THE LAUNCH OF THE KONY2012 PR CAMPAIGN.
BUT WAS ACELLAM TRULY CAPTURED? OR HAD HE BEEN COOPERATING WITH THE UGANDANS ALL ALONG?
THERE WERE TWO VERSIONS OF ACELLAM'S STORY, EACH SUPPORTING A DIFFERENT VIEW OF THE INTERNATIONAL CAMPAIGN TO DEFEAT THE LRA.
WHITE HOUSE PRESS SECRETARY JAY CARNEY
THE CAPTURE OF MAJOR GENERAL CEASAR ACELLAM IS A TESTAMENT TO THE RESOLVE OF UGANDA AND ITS MILITARY FORCES TO WORK WITH REGIONAL FORCES TO END THE THREAT POSED BY THE LRA.
THE OFFICIAL POSITION WAS CLEAR ENOUGH: ACELLAM WAS A REBEL LEADER, AND HIS CAPTURE A BATTLEFIELD VICTORY FOR THE FORCES OF GOOD.
BUT ANOTHER NARRATIVE WAS EVIDENT IN THE DETAILS.
IT WAS POSSIBLE ACELLAM HAD LONG AGO LEFT THE LRA, AND HAD AGREED TO APPEAR FOR THE CAMERAS TO BOOST THE IMAGE OF A DIFFICULT, AND PERHAPS DOOMED, MILITARY CAMPAIGN.

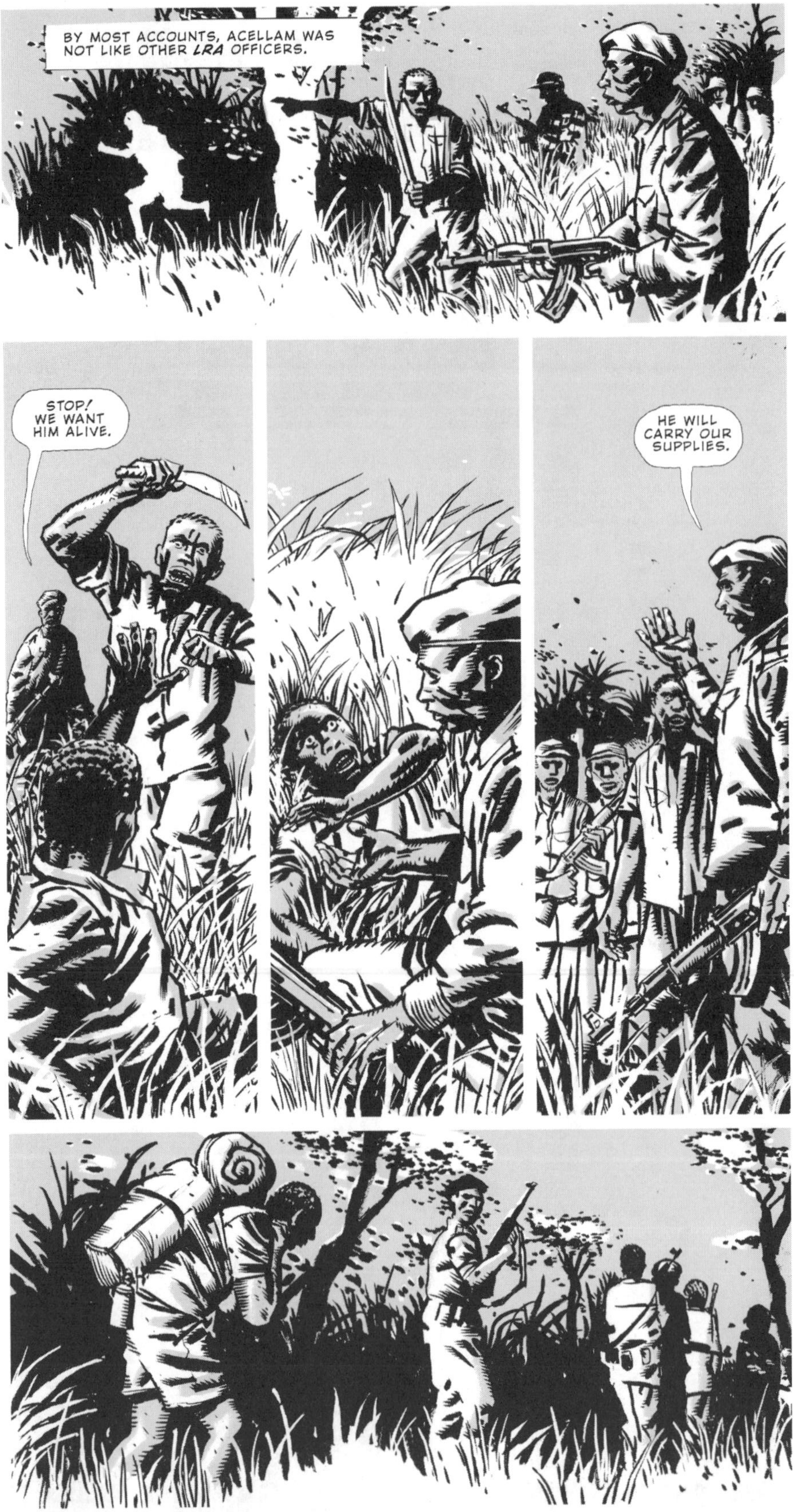
BY MOST ACCOUNTS, ACELLAM WAS NOT LIKE OTHER *LRA* OFFICERS.
STOP! WE WANT HIM ALIVE.
HE WILL CARRY OUR SUPPLIES.

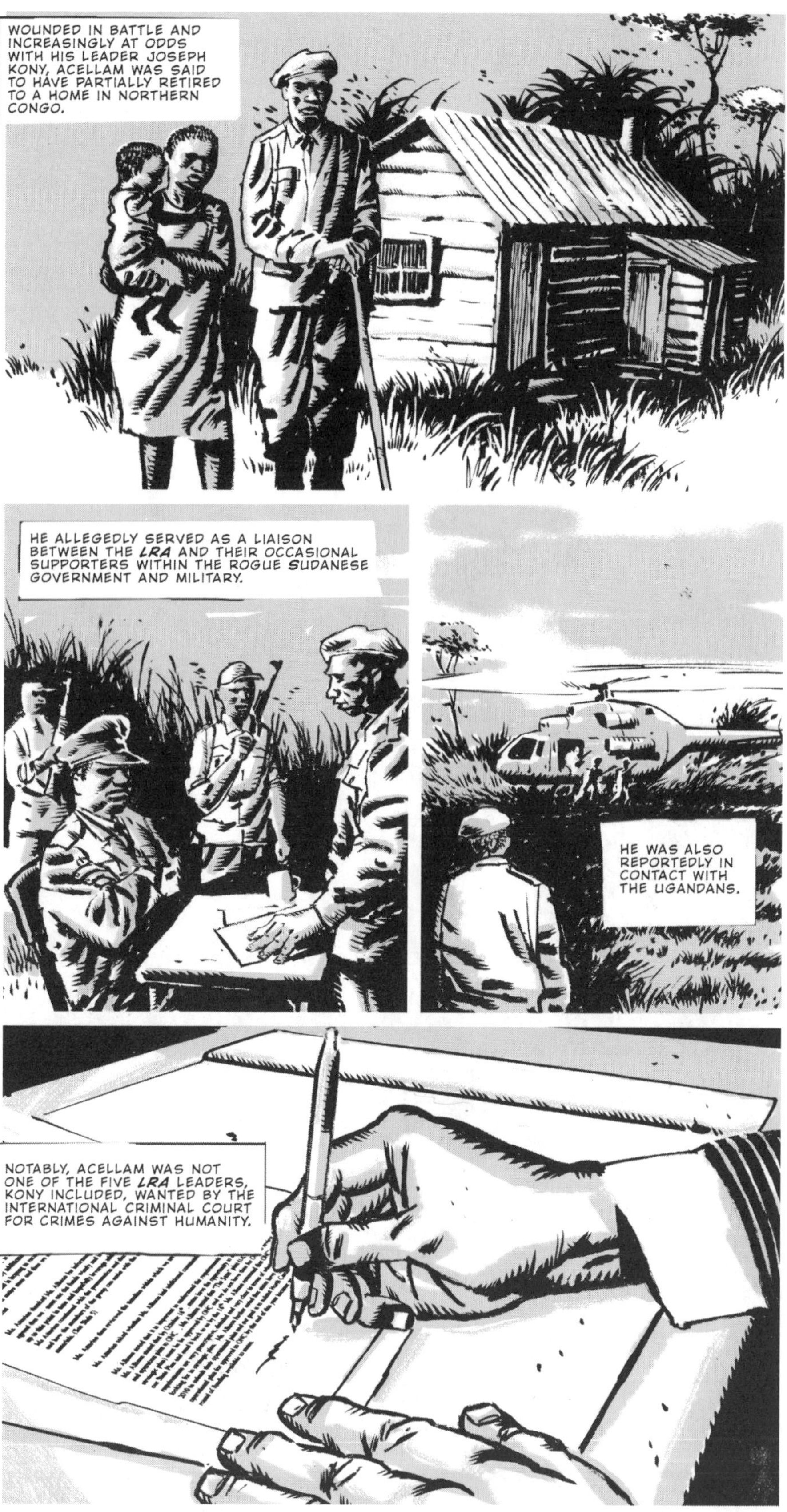
WOUNDED IN BATTLE AND INCREASINGLY AT ODDS WITH HIS LEADER JOSEPH KONY, ACELLAM WAS SAID TO HAVE PARTIALLY RETIRED TO A HOME IN NORTHERN CONGO.
HE ALLEGEDLY SERVED AS A LIAISON BETWEEN THE *LRA* AND THEIR OCCASIONAL SUPPORTERS WITHIN THE ROGUE SUDANESE GOVERNMENT AND MILITARY.
HE WAS ALSO REPORTEDLY IN CONTACT WITH THE UGANDANS.
NOTABLY, ACELLAM WAS NOT ONE OF THE FIVE *LRA* LEADERS, KONY INCLUDED, WANTED BY THE INTERNATIONAL CRIMINAL COURT FOR CRIMES AGAINST HUMANITY.

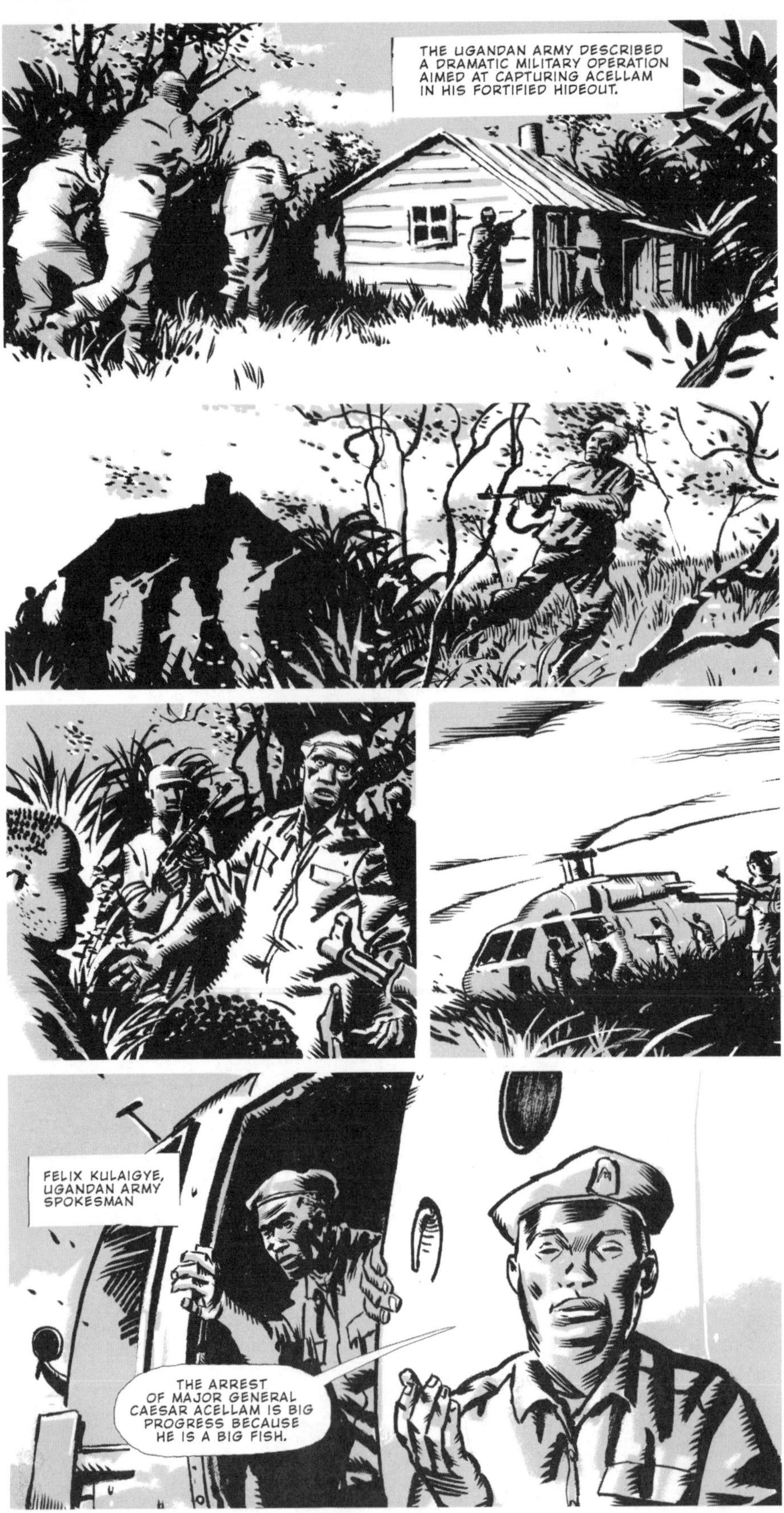
THE UGANDAN ARMY DESCRIBED A DRAMATIC MILITARY OPERATION AIMED AT CAPTURING ACELLAM IN HIS FORTIFIED HIDEOUT.
FELIX KULAIGYE, UGANDAN ARMY SPOKESMAN
THE ARREST OF MAJOR GENERAL CAESAR ACELLAM IS BIG PROGRESS BECAUSE HE IS A BIG FISH.

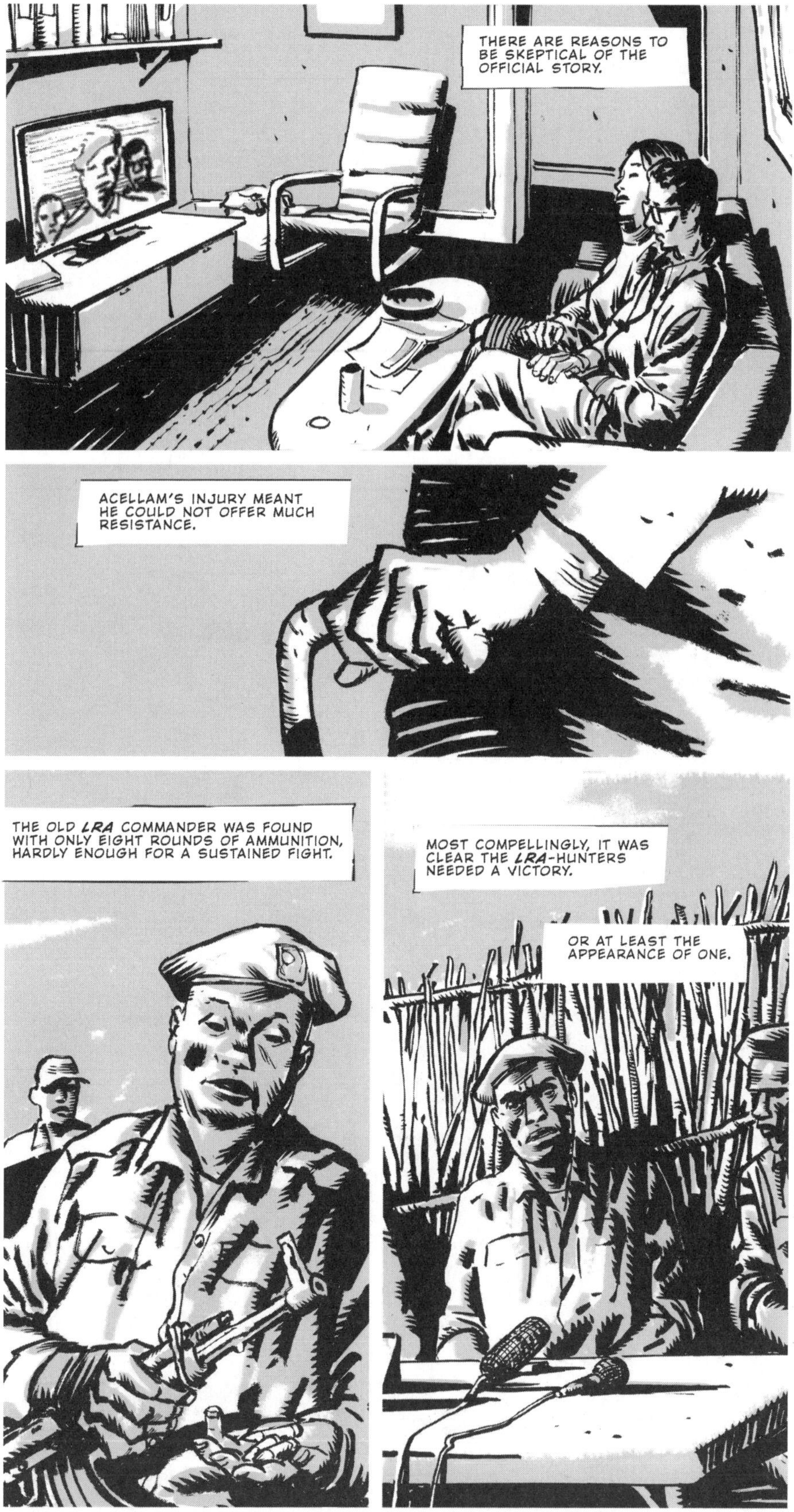
THERE ARE REASONS TO BE SKEPTICAL OF THE OFFICIAL STORY.
ACELLAM'S INJURY MEANT HE COULD NOT OFFER MUCH RESISTANCE.
THE OLD *LRA* COMMANDER WAS FOUND WITH ONLY EIGHT ROUNDS OF AMMUNITION, HARDLY ENOUGH FOR A SUSTAINED FIGHT.
MOST COMPELLINGLY, IT WAS CLEAR THE *LRA*-HUNTERS NEEDED A VICTORY.
OR AT LEAST THE APPEARANCE OF ONE.

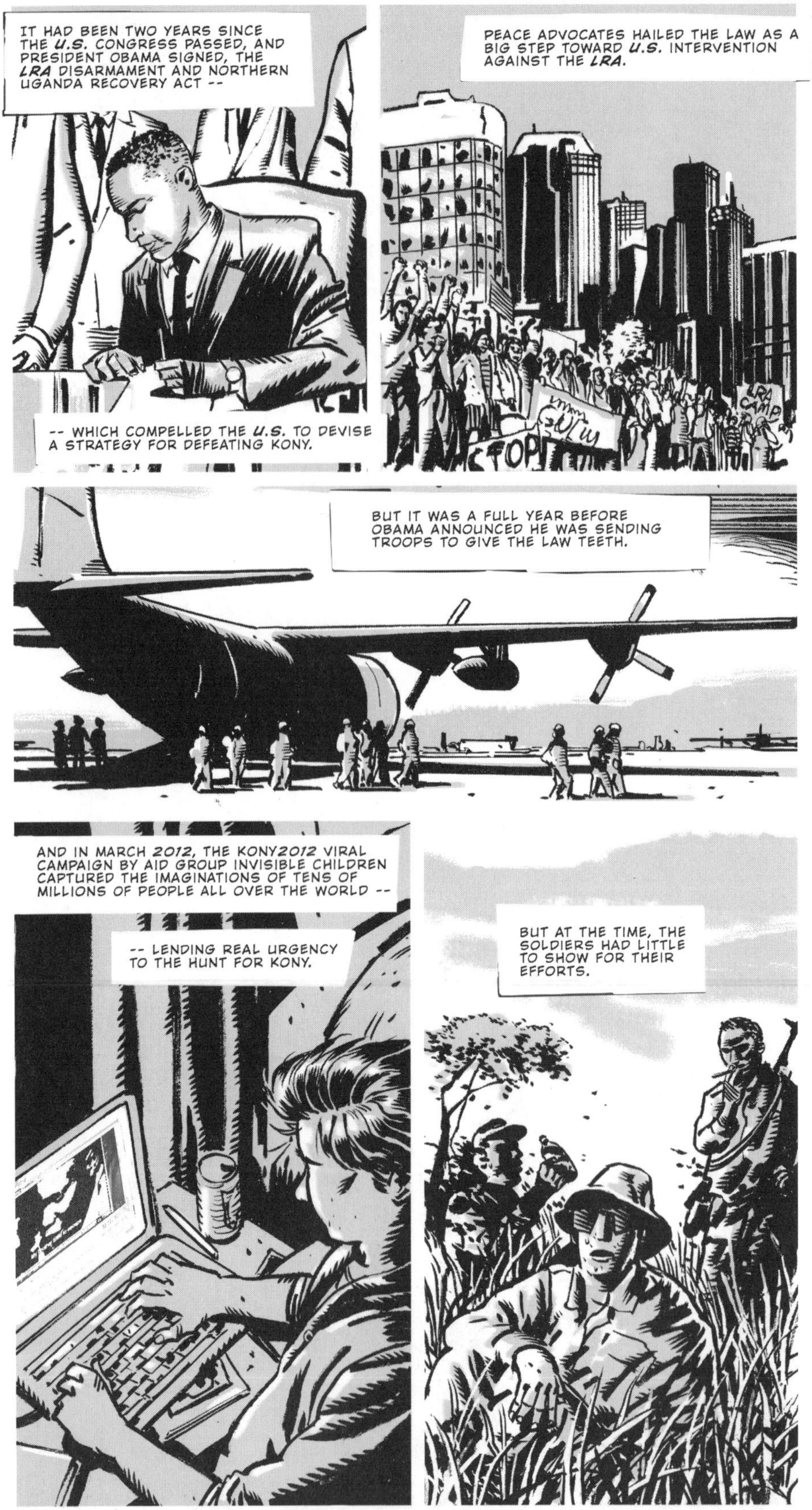
IT HAD BEEN TWO YEARS SINCE THE *U.S.* CONGRESS PASSED, AND PRESIDENT OBAMA SIGNED, THE *LRA* DISARMAMENT AND NORTHERN UGANDA RECOVERY ACT --
-- WHICH COMPELLED THE *U.S.* TO DEVISE A STRATEGY FOR DEFEATING KONY.
PEACE ADVOCATES HAILED THE LAW AS A BIG STEP TOWARD *U.S.* INTERVENTION AGAINST THE *LRA*.
BUT IT WAS A FULL YEAR BEFORE OBAMA ANNOUNCED HE WAS SENDING TROOPS TO GIVE THE LAW TEETH.
AND IN MARCH *2012*, THE KONY*2012* VIRAL CAMPAIGN BY AID GROUP INVISIBLE CHILDREN CAPTURED THE IMAGINATIONS OF TENS OF MILLIONS OF PEOPLE ALL OVER THE WORLD --
-- LENDING REAL URGENCY TO THE HUNT FOR KONY.
BUT AT THE TIME, THE SOLDIERS HAD LITTLE TO SHOW FOR THEIR EFFORTS.

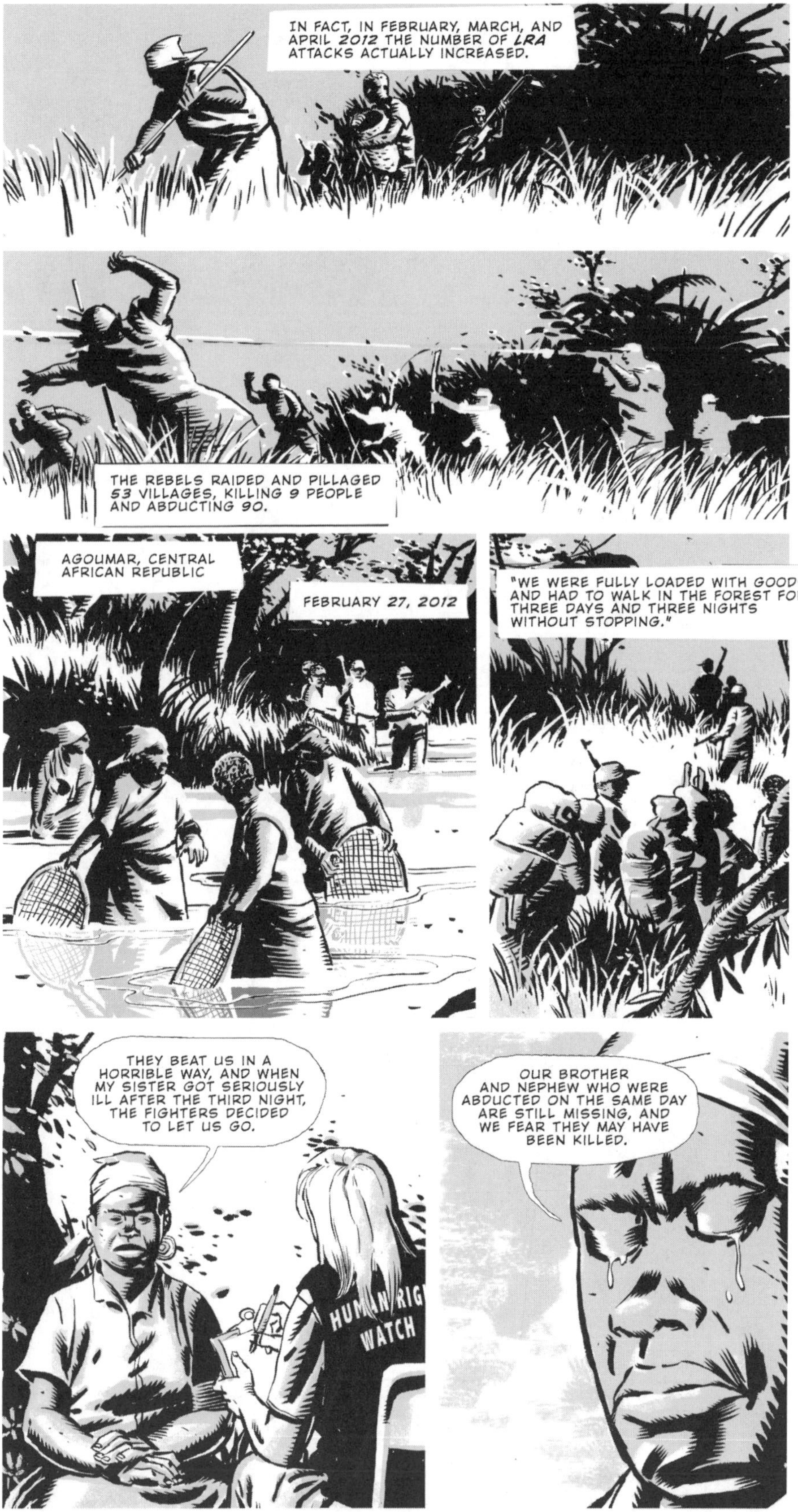
IN FACT, IN FEBRUARY, MARCH, AND APRIL 2012 THE NUMBER OF LRA ATTACKS ACTUALLY INCREASED.
THE REBELS RAIDED AND PILLAGED 53 VILLAGES, KILLING 9 PEOPLE AND ABDUCTING 90.
AGOUMAR, CENTRAL AFRICAN REPUBLIC
FEBRUARY 27, 2012
"WE WERE FULLY LOADED WITH GOODS AND HAD TO WALK IN THE FOREST FOR THREE DAYS AND THREE NIGHTS WITHOUT STOPPING."
THEY BEAT US IN A HORRIBLE WAY, AND WHEN MY SISTER GOT SERIOUSLY ILL AFTER THE THIRD NIGHT, THE FIGHTERS DECIDED TO LET US GO.
HUMAN RIG
WATCH
OUR BROTHER AND NEPHEW WHO WERE ABDUCTED ON THE SAME DAY ARE STILL MISSING, AND WE FEAR THEY MAY HAVE BEEN KILLED.

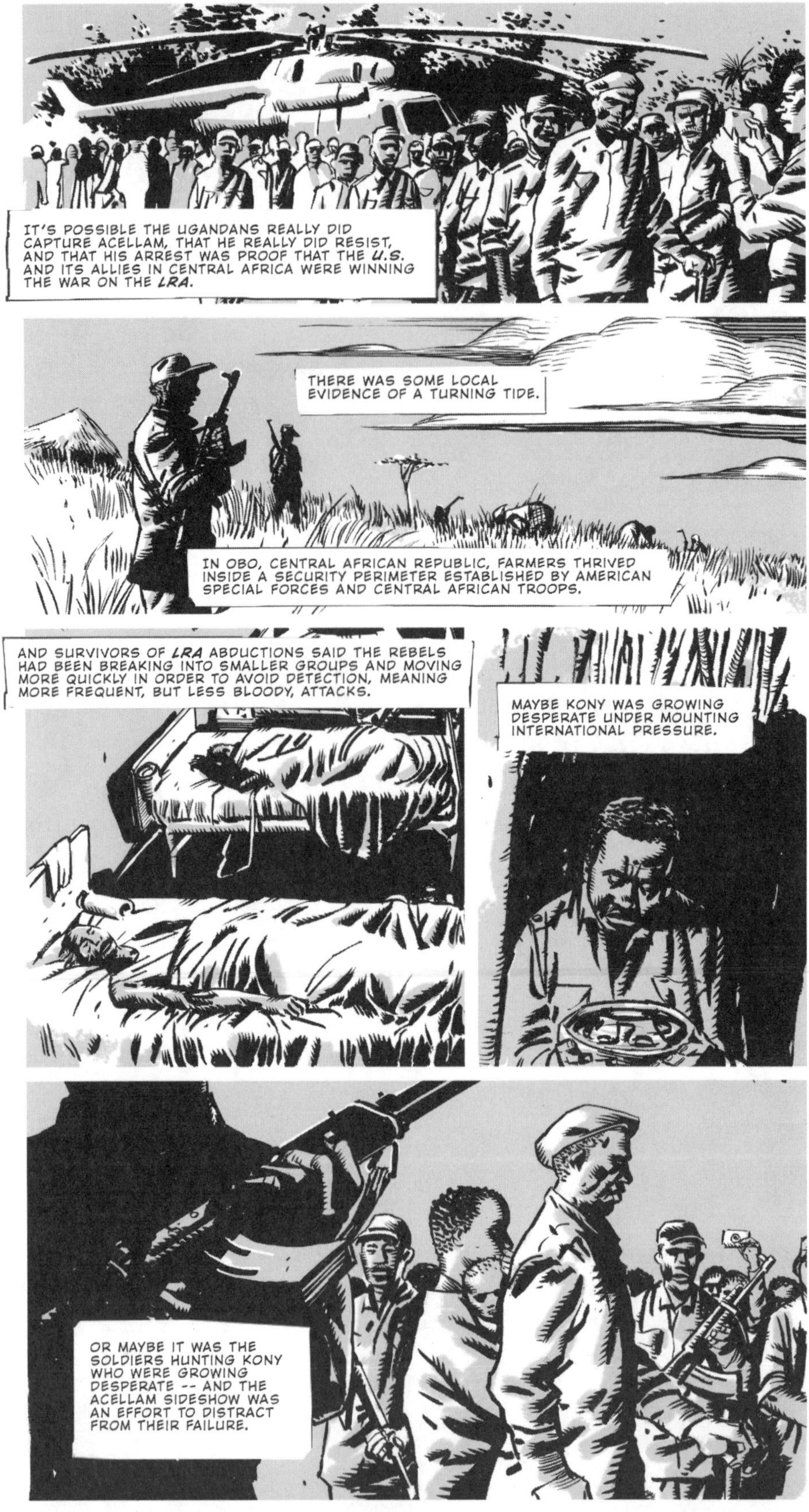
IT'S POSSIBLE THE UGANDANS REALLY DID CAPTURE ACELLAM, THAT HE REALLY DID RESIST, AND THAT HIS ARREST WAS PROOF THAT THE U.S. AND ITS ALLIES IN CENTRAL AFRICA WERE WINNING THE WAR ON THE LRA.
THERE WAS SOME LOCAL EVIDENCE OF A TURNING TIDE.
IN OBO, CENTRAL AFRICAN REPUBLIC, FARMERS THRIVED INSIDE A SECURITY PERIMETER ESTABLISHED BY AMERICAN SPECIAL FORCES AND CENTRAL AFRICAN TROOPS.
AND SURVIVORS OF LRA ABDUCTIONS SAID THE REBELS HAD BEEN BREAKING INTO SMALLER GROUPS AND MOVING MORE QUICKLY IN ORDER TO AVOID DETECTION, MEANING MORE FREQUENT, BUT LESS BLOODY, ATTACKS.
MAYBE KONY WAS GROWING DESPERATE UNDER MOUNTING INTERNATIONAL PRESSURE.
OR MAYBE IT WAS THE SOLDIERS HUNTING KONY WHO WERE GROWING DESPERATE -- AND THE ACELLAM SIDESHOW WAS AN EFFORT TO DISTRACT FROM THEIR FAILURE.

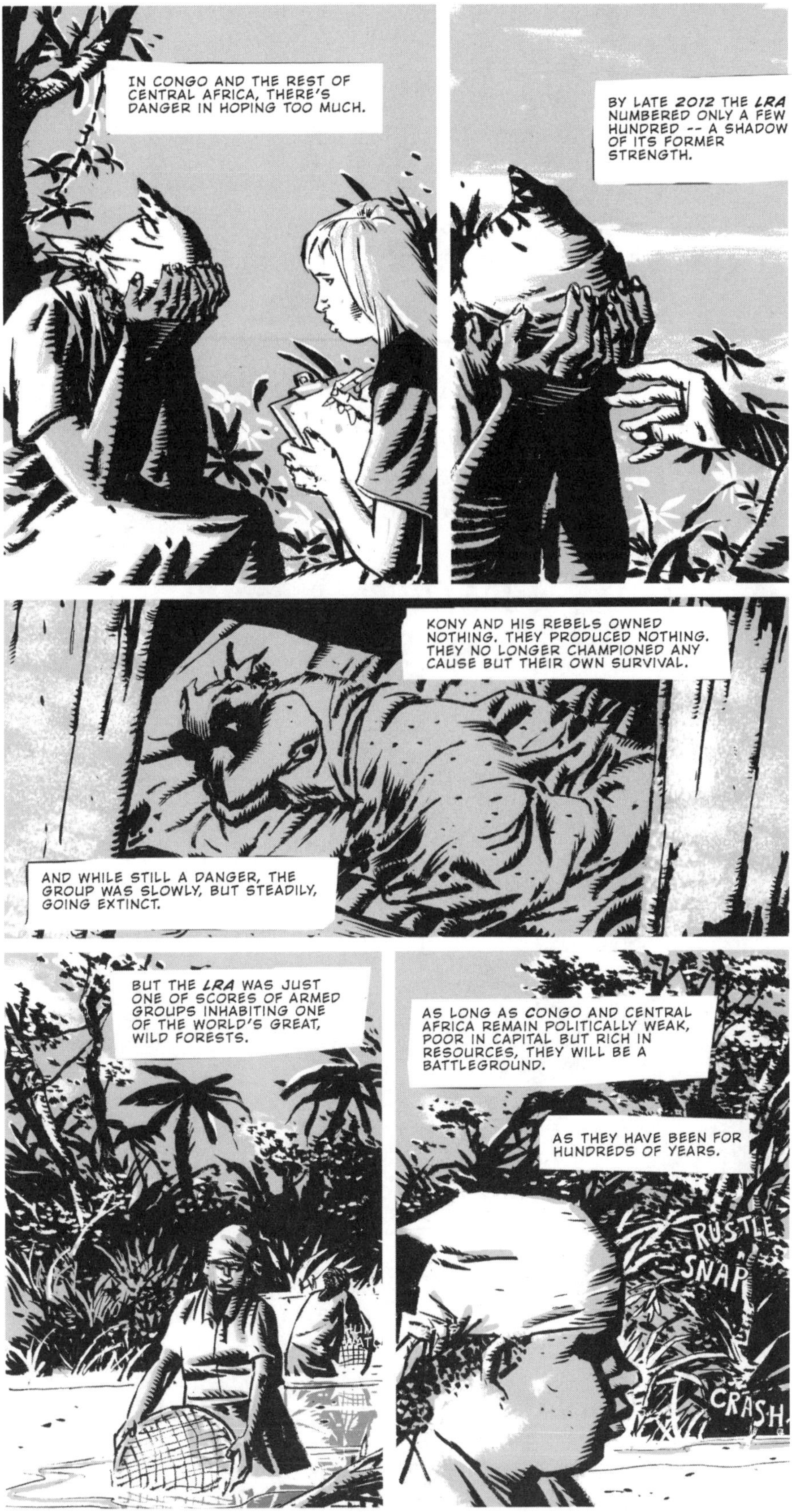
IN CONGO AND THE REST OF CENTRAL AFRICA, THERE'S DANGER IN HOPING TOO MUCH.
BY LATE *2012* THE *LRA* NUMBERED ONLY A FEW HUNDRED -- A SHADOW OF ITS FORMER STRENGTH.
KONY AND HIS REBELS OWNED NOTHING. THEY PRODUCED NOTHING. THEY NO LONGER CHAMPIONED ANY CAUSE BUT THEIR OWN SURVIVAL.
AND WHILE STILL A DANGER, THE GROUP WAS SLOWLY, BUT STEADILY, GOING EXTINCT.
BUT THE *LRA* WAS JUST ONE OF SCORES OF ARMED GROUPS INHABITING ONE OF THE WORLD'S GREAT, WILD FORESTS.
AS LONG AS CONGO AND CENTRAL AFRICA REMAIN POLITICALLY WEAK, POOR IN CAPITAL BUT RICH IN RESOURCES, THEY WILL BE A BATTLEGROUND.
AS THEY HAVE BEEN FOR HUNDREDS OF YEARS.
RUSTLE
SNAP
CRASH

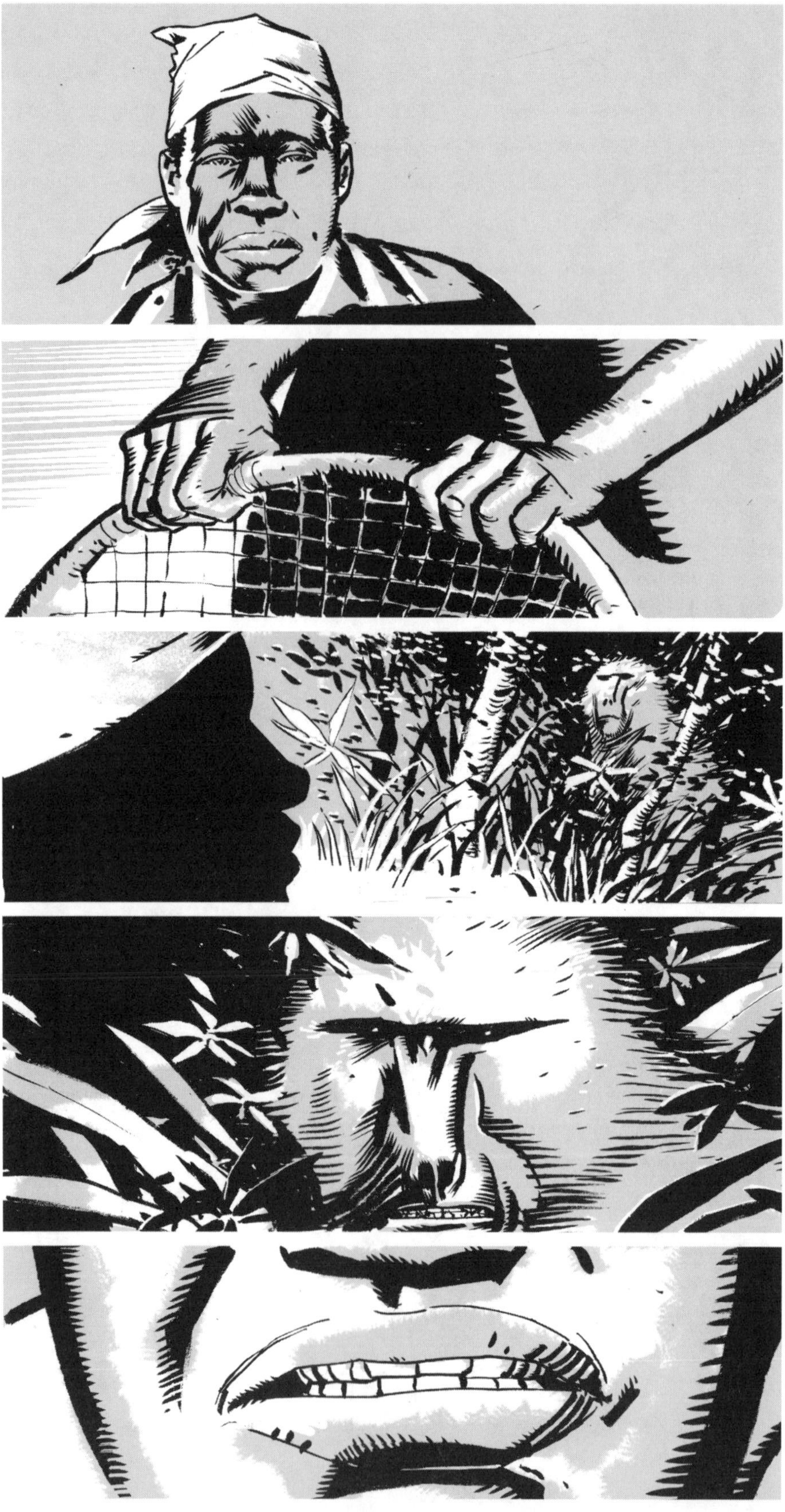

EPILOGUE

AT THE TIME of this writing—November 2012—Joseph Kony remains at large, most likely somewhere in Central African Republic. He and his fighters are being hunted by a combined 2,500 U.S., Ugandan, Congolese, South Sudanese, and Central African troops plus thousands of U.N. peacekeepers. Equipped with helicopters and armored vehicles and supported by American spy planes and drones, the international army pursuing the LRA is among the deadliest ever to take to the field in Subsaharan Africa.

But the coalition's fearsomeness belies the difficulty of its task. Kony and his men are spread out in small groups across hundreds of thousands of square miles of dense forest. They move quickly, pillage defenseless villages for supplies, and kill anyone who stands in their way. The rebels do not seek a confrontation with the armies chasing them. The only way to catch the LRA is to corner it.

For that reason some humanitarians worry the LRA leader may never be caught. The coalition could collapse before it manages to run down Kony and his rebels. The U.S.-based Enough Project, which has collaborated with Invisible Children on counter-LRA efforts, said the military operations are "unsustainable."

Case in point, in the summer and fall of 2012 the government of the Democratic Republic of Congo and the U.N. were forced to shift their troops' focus away from the LRA in order to deal with a rebellion by former Congolese soldiers. The so-called "M23" movement, led by a wanted war criminal and allegedly backed by Rwanda and Uganda, captured several key towns in eastern Congo and tied down hundreds, if not thousands, of Congolese and U.N. troops in running gun battles that killed scores of people and displaced thousands.

When the U.N. accused Uganda of supplying the M23 rebels, the government in Kampala threatened to pull its troops from the Kony hunt. Likewise, the U.S. has signaled it may end military collaboration with Uganda over the latter's escalating oppression of gays and lesbians. Issues unrelated to the LRA mission may end up tearing the military coalition apart.

Granted, over time the scale and location of LRA activities has shifted, somewhat reducing the importance of both Congo and Uganda in the Kony manhunt. The LRA has been moving north, toward the Central African Republic and South Sudan, increasing the burden on those countries to sustain security partnerships and protect their populations. That said, the Ugandans have the best army in the region and the most experience battling the LRA. Losing Uganda would be be major blow to the Kony-hunters.

Fortunately, the LRA appears to be shriveling. From a peak of several thousand fighters a decade ago, in recent years Kony's rebels have numbered just a few hundred. In a 2010 diplomatic cable that was leaked to the press, the U.S. State Department estimated there were up to 600 LRA fighters divided into six groups. Ugandan army spokesman Felix Kulayigye insisted the number was much lower: fewer than 100. The State Department cited another military source indicating that just 80 of Kony's rebels remained in the DRC.

Which is not to say the LRA is no longer dangerous. In fact, its surviving members appear to be more aggressive that ever. Maybe it's a sign of desperation on the part of Kony's rebels. Maybe it's proof that, when it comes to the LRA, it doesn't take many people to terrorize an entire region.

According to a joint report by Invisible Children and Enough, there were 155 LRA attacks in Congo in the first half of 2012, compared to just half that number in 2011. Over the same period there were 35 suspected LRA raids in Central African Republic, as many as occurred in all of 2011. On September 1, 2012, in Balifondo, a town in southern CAR, a group of 20 LRA abducted 55 people including 14 young girls, and severely beat 19 people.

Since 2008 the U.S. has spent $30 million a year trying to defeat Kony and his fighters. But even that might not be enough. "We have to get the equipment and resources that will help rid the world of this terrible man," Secretary of State Hillary Clinton said during an August 2012 visit to a U.S. Special Forces base in Uganda. Clinton observed a demonstration flight by a small surveillance drone, but worried it would not be able to detect the nimble LRA fighters through the forest canopy. "We have to figure out one that can go through thick vegetation to get Kony," Clinton said.

But all the high-tech gear in the world might not make much difference. The Americans lack the experience to track fleet-footed fighters in the Central African wilderness. That's a job best left to local forces, particularly the ambivalent Ugandans. "They are the experts," said Daniel Travis, a State Department spokesman. "They are the ones who have been chasing Kony for a long time."

Ugandan spokesman Kulayigye agreed, "This is not a war for the Americans." But if the Ugandans quit the fight, as they have threatened to do, the U.S. may have no choice but to increase its own involvement. The alternative could be giving up.

Despite the obstacles and uncertainty, some observers remain optimistic. John Campbell from the Council on Foreign Relations said he believes Kony will be caught and LRA destroyed. His concern, he said, is what happens next. "The scary thought is that once he is caught and the Lord's Resistance Army is dissolved, is it to be replaced by something else like it?"

No one knows.

SOURCES

Foreign Policy: http://turtlebay.foreignpolicy.com/posts/2012/11/09/uganda_threatens_to_quit_hunt_for_joseph_kony

Invisible Children, Enough Project, via HSBA: http://www.smallarms surveysudan.org/facts-figures/south-sudan/armed-groups/lra.html

The Los Angeles Times: http://www.latimes.com/news/world/worldnow/la-fg-wn-lords-resistance-army-20121113,0,4634685.story

The Washington Post: http://www.washingtonpost.com/world/africa/group-says-hunt-for-warlord-kony-hopeless-without-more-troops-increased-american-involvement/2012/11/09/b43ec6c2-2a52-11e2-aaa5-ac786110c486_story.html

DRAMATIS PERSONAE

FIDEL MBOLIGIKPELE

A schoolteacher in Duru when the LRA attacked in 2008, Fidel lost almost his entire class to the rebels. Fleeing to nearby Dungu, Fidel became a teacher for internally-displaced refugees and a vocal advocate for international intervention against the LRA, even speaking to U.S. Secretary of State Hillary Clinton and U.N. envoy Angelina Jolie in a three-way video that was broadcast internationally. I met him at his home in a refugee camp on the outskirts of town, where he lived with his ailing father in a mud hut.

FERRUCCIO GOBBI

A septuagenarian Italian priest in Duru, eastern Congo, who was abducted by the LRA during a bloody assault on the town in September 2008. I met Gobbi two years later in nearby Dungu, where he and many other Duru survivors relocated after their release or liberation from the LRA. Gobbi was a quiet, soft-spoken, and methodical man who happily offered me vital testimony, notes, and photos recalling the LRA's recent terror campaign. Photo: courtesy Ferruccio Gobbi

"PATRICIA"

Quiet, shy, and stunningly beautiful, "Patricia"—not her real name—was just 13 years old when I met her in Dungu, eastern Congo, in late 2010. A year earlier her father had been killed by LRA fighters and she and her brother had been kidnapped and enslaved by the group. She was liberated by Ugandan troops, but found returning to normal life difficult.

ERNEST SUGULE

 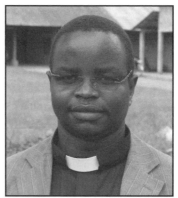

A cheerful young Catholic priest in eastern Congo who headed local efforts to reintegrate girls and women victimized by the LRA—a difficult task in a culture that tends to blame sexual violence on the victim. I met Father Ernest in Dungu, where he quickly became my unofficial guide and interpreter of Congolese dialects.

"JOSEPH"

A resident of Obo in Central African Republic near the border with Congo, "Joseph"—not his real name—helped lead the village's self-defense militia. Armed with homemade shotguns, Joseph and his militiamen patrolled the forest to ward off raids by the LRA. The village's defenses improved greatly when aid group Invisible Children installed a radio for contacting U.N. and government forces.

JOSEPH KABILA

President of the Democratic Republic of Congo since the 2001 assassination of his father Laurent-Desiree. Born in a rebel encampment where his father was a leading revolutionary, Joseph was just 30 years old when he took office. His rule coincided with economic, democratic, diplomatic, and military reforms, but Congo remained a country wracked by rebellion and plagued by the LRA.

JOSEPH KONY

The deadly, mercurial founder and leader of the Lord's Resistance Army, a once-Ugandan armed group chased from its home country and currently on the run in Central Africa. Born in 1961 in war-torn northern Uganda, Kony fell under the sway of apocalyptic religious leaders and, in 1986, gathered followers for his own rebellion. The LRA killed thousands and forced many others to fight, work, or bear children for the group. From a peak of thousands of fighters, by 2012 the LRA had dwindled to just a few hundred.

CAESAR ACELLAM

A one-time top lieutenant in Joseph Kony's Lord's Resistance Army who reportedly was living in a state of semi-retirement in northeastern Congo when he was either captured by, or gave himself up to, Ugandan troops on the border with the Central African Republic in mid-2012.

GEORGE W. BUSH

As U.S. president from 2001 to 2009, Bush launched the slowly escalating American intervention in the Central African conflict, initially by providing indirect military support to Ugandan troops battling the LRA. Bush's successor, Barack Obama, significantly expanded on the early efforts.

HILLARY CLINTON

As secretary of state under U.S. President Barack Obama, Clinton made Central Africa a much higher priority. Her tour of Congo and neighboring countries in 2009 laid the groundwork for U.S. aid, diplomatic support, and direct military intervention.

BARACK OBAMA

The U.S. president beginning in early 2009, Obama built on the nascent Congo intervention launched by outgoing President George W. Bush. Obama added money and military trainers and, after signing a law requiring the U.S. to develop a strategy for defeating the LRA, sent 100 Special Forces troops specially to help hunt the rebels in Uganda, Congo, Central African Republic, and South Sudan.

JASON RUSSELL

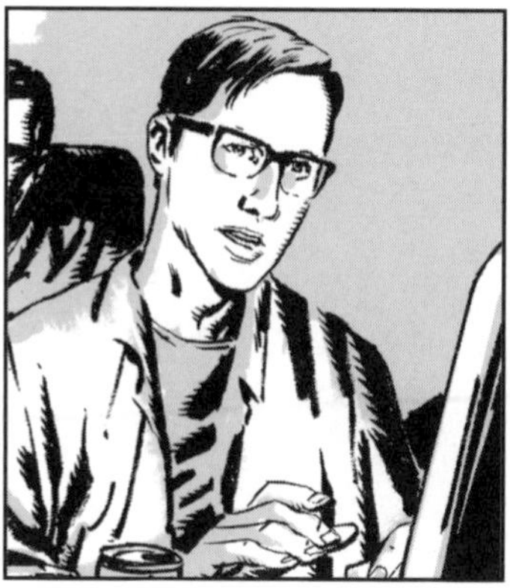

One of the founding members of San Diego-based aid group Invisible Children, Russell was the driving creative force behind the group's slick advocacy videos. I met Invisible Children members in eastern Congo in late 2010 as they were developing their plans for helping defeat the LRA. Russell's "Kony2012" video calling for international action against the LRA leader debuted in March 2012 and quickly went viral. With millions of people watching, Russell cracked under the strain.

A NOTE ON PROCESS

FOR ANY NONFICTION GRAPHIC NOVEL—and I've written several—I begin with a foundation of reporting. In practice, reporting for comics is no different than reporting in any other medium. For *Army of God*, I first conducted interviews with experts and analysts in the U.S. In September 2010 I traveled to Kinshasa for more interviews with government officials, diplomats, soldiers, aid workers, and everyday people, and to observe firsthand a U.S. military training exercise with the Congolese army. After a couple weeks in the capital, I flew east to the Dungu—LRA country— and repeated the process.

The result was a body of material that I then had to translate into a script. I began by outlining the overall, recent arc of the Congo conflict, beginning with a broad historical overview. Within that arc I lined up several individual tales, each focusing on a particular participant in the conflict. The final script ended up looking a lot like a screenplay, with scene descriptions and dialogue.

I handed the script over to Tim Hamilton. He had already produced a few preliminary sketches, as seen on the following pages, in order to develop the book's style. With script in hand, he began churning out inked and lettered pages. He'd send them back to me for copy editing—that is, checking grammar and spelling—but I rarely had to correct anything. Tim is thorough. I never needed to ask for major changes to the art. If you have a good artist, it's best to trust him and give him the freedom to make his own decisions.

Army of God began as an online comic, serialized on the Website of Cartoon Movement, a Dutch organization that supports editorial cartooning and comics journalism. Tim produced roughly a chapter a month from January to August 2012. That's fast. For PublicAffairs' print edition, I wrote additional chapters of fresh material and Tim did his usual excellent job drawing them. The book you hold in your hands reflects Tim's speed and professionalism, and the more than two years I've spent researching, traveling to, and writing about Congo, Joseph Kony, and the Lord's Resistance Army.

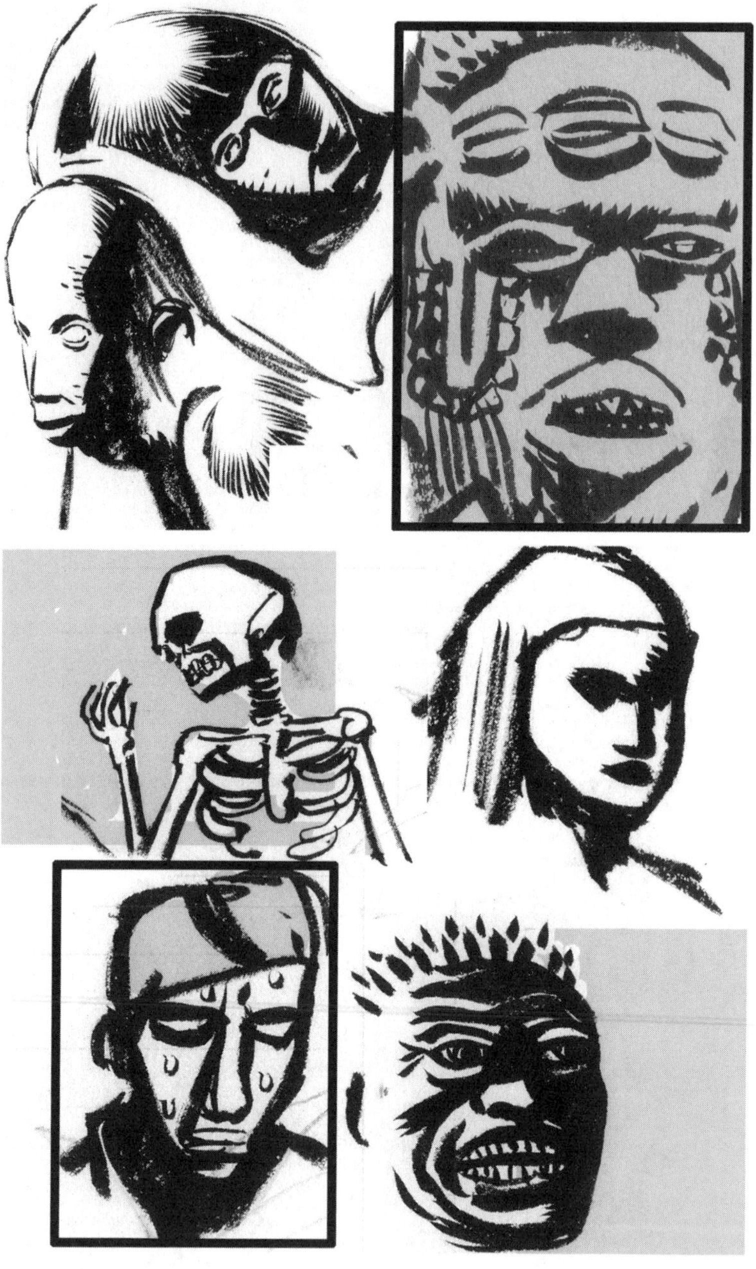

Before he even had a script for *Army of God*, Tim headed to the Metropolitan Museum of Art to fill his head with the motifs and designs of Africa. Much of this art didn't appear in the book, but the time spent sketching was valuable even so.

After getting a script Tim experimented with drawing some of the personalities in the book. He knew he wanted to illustrate the book with a brush as opposed to a pen, but he tried out smaller brushes and large Japanese Pentel brush pens along the way. These are early sketches of Mobutu and two different sketches of Laurent-Desire Kabila.

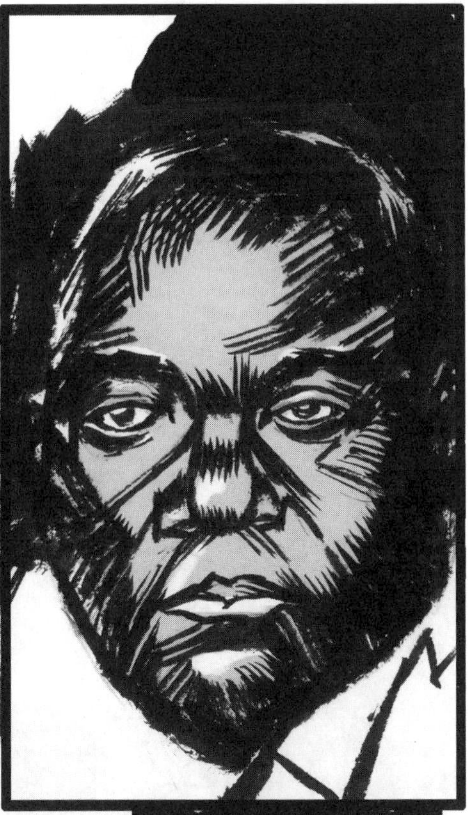

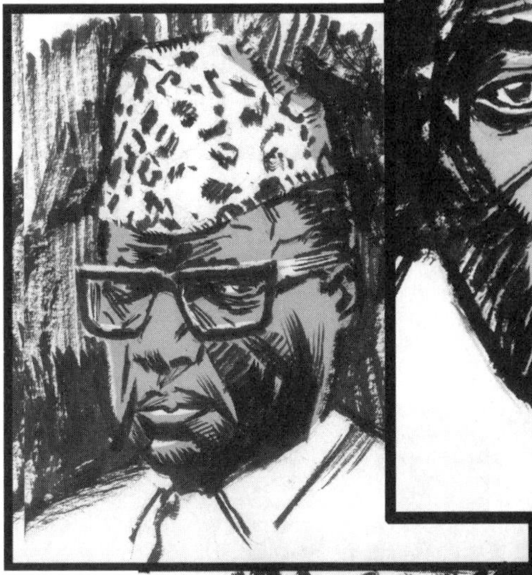

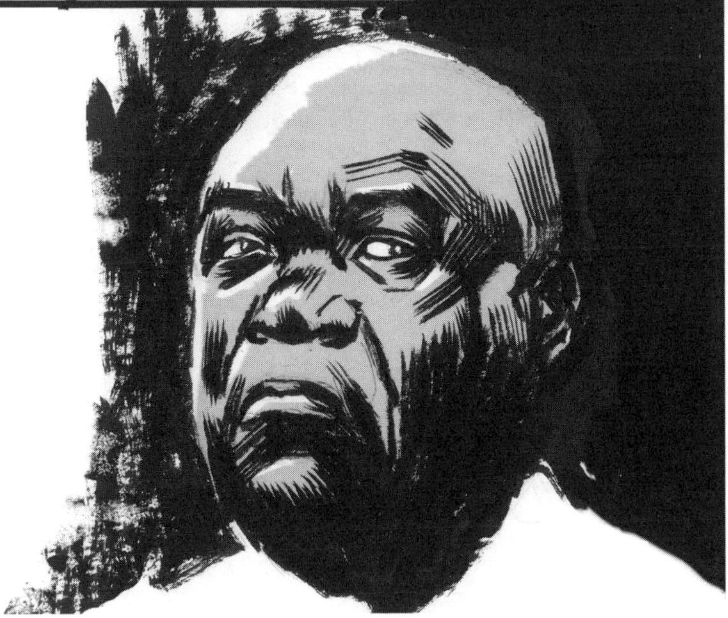

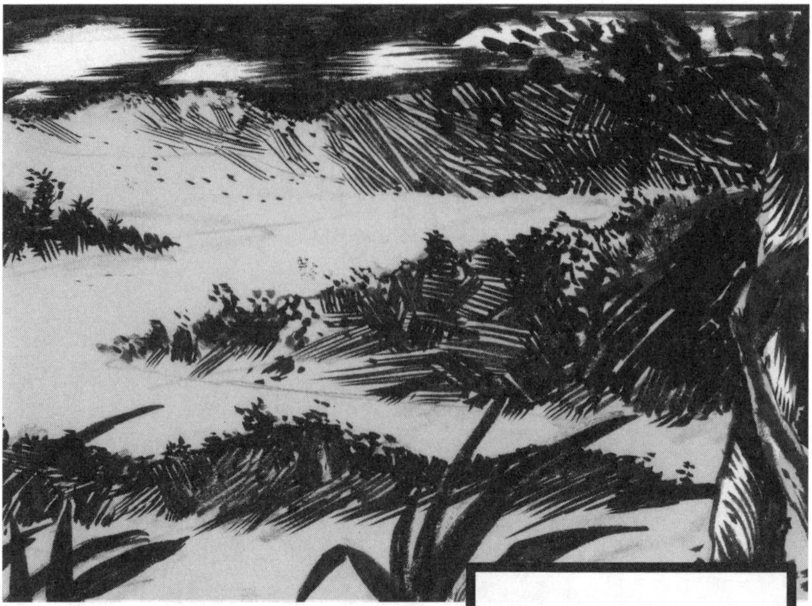

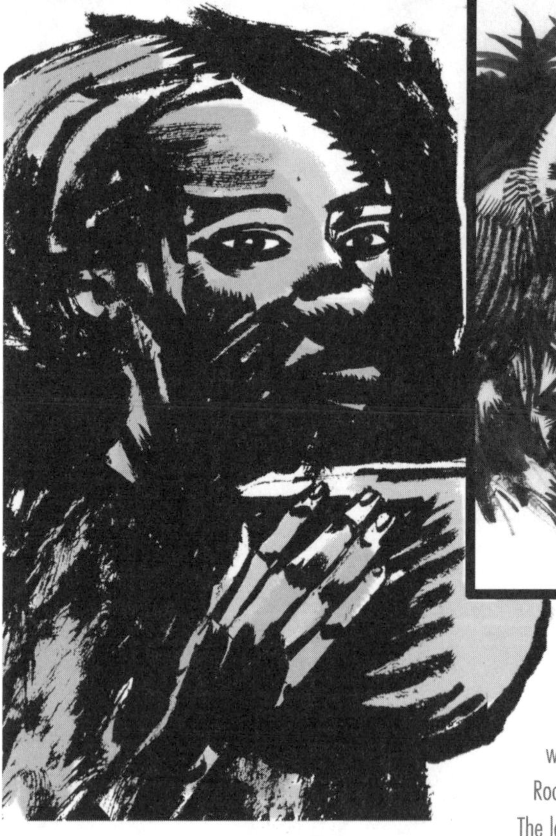

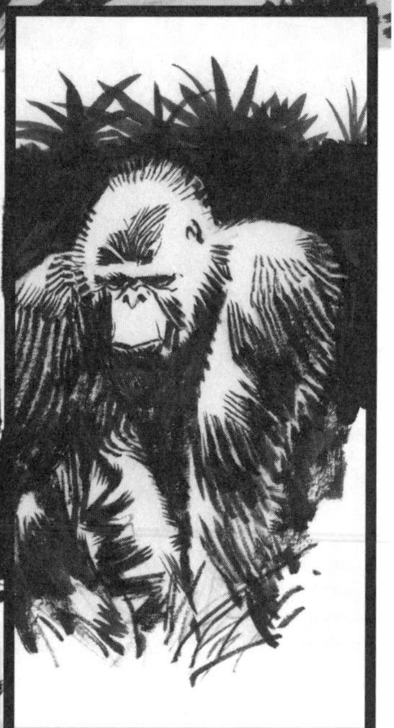

Tim tried using a very large brush for some sketches, seen above, as well as smaller brushes to draw landscapes. Tim was looking at wood block artists such as Rockwell Kent to influence the look of the art. The loose, rough look of the brush would reflect the "rough" disturbing content of the story.

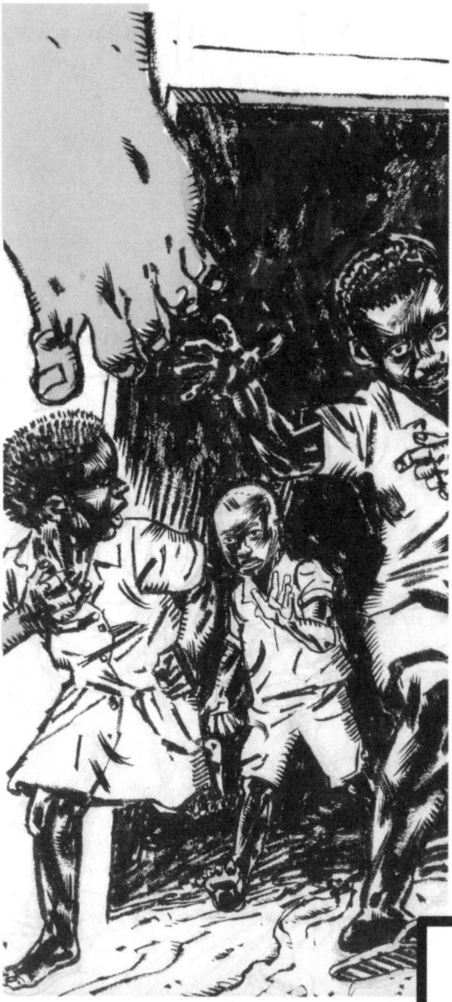

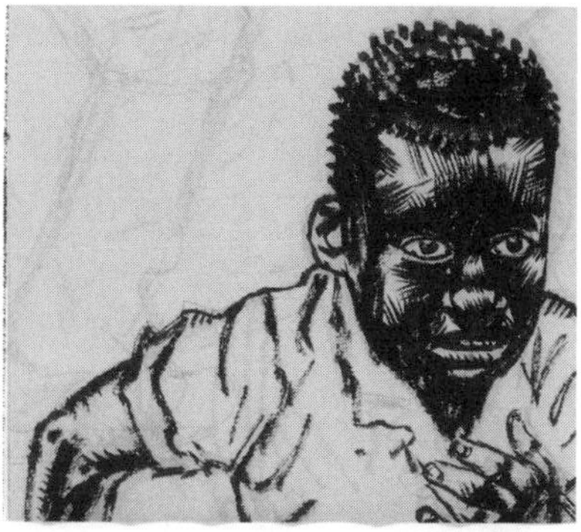

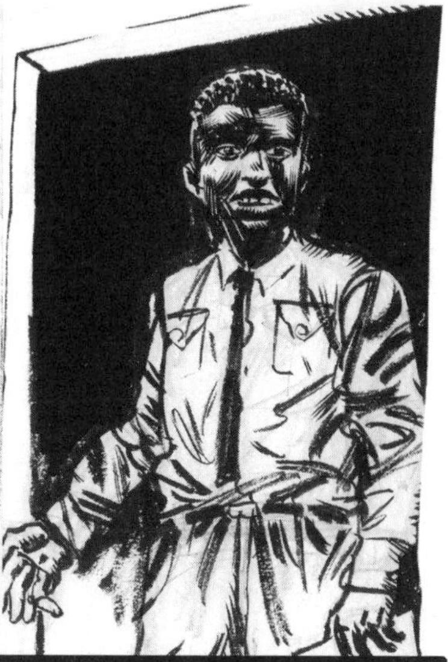

One of Tim's test pages can be seen above. He rejected this page as he felt the brush work was too heavy and distracting. The sketches below and to the right came closer to the art's final look.

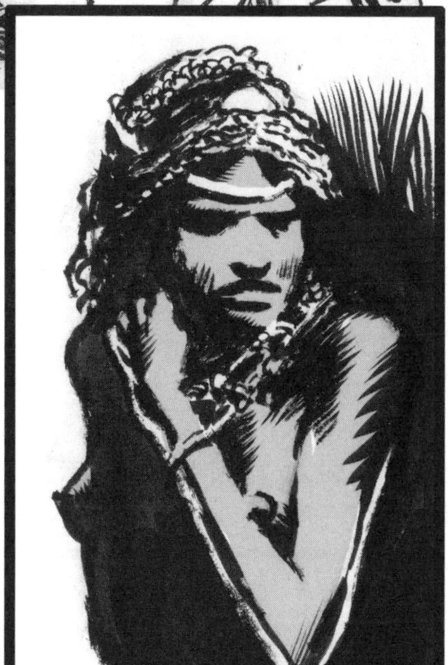

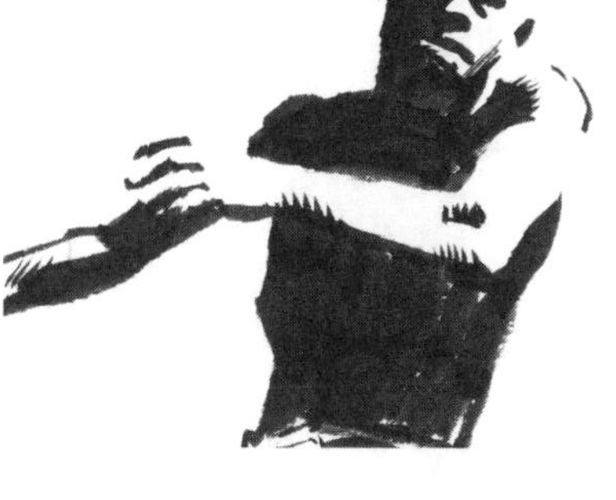

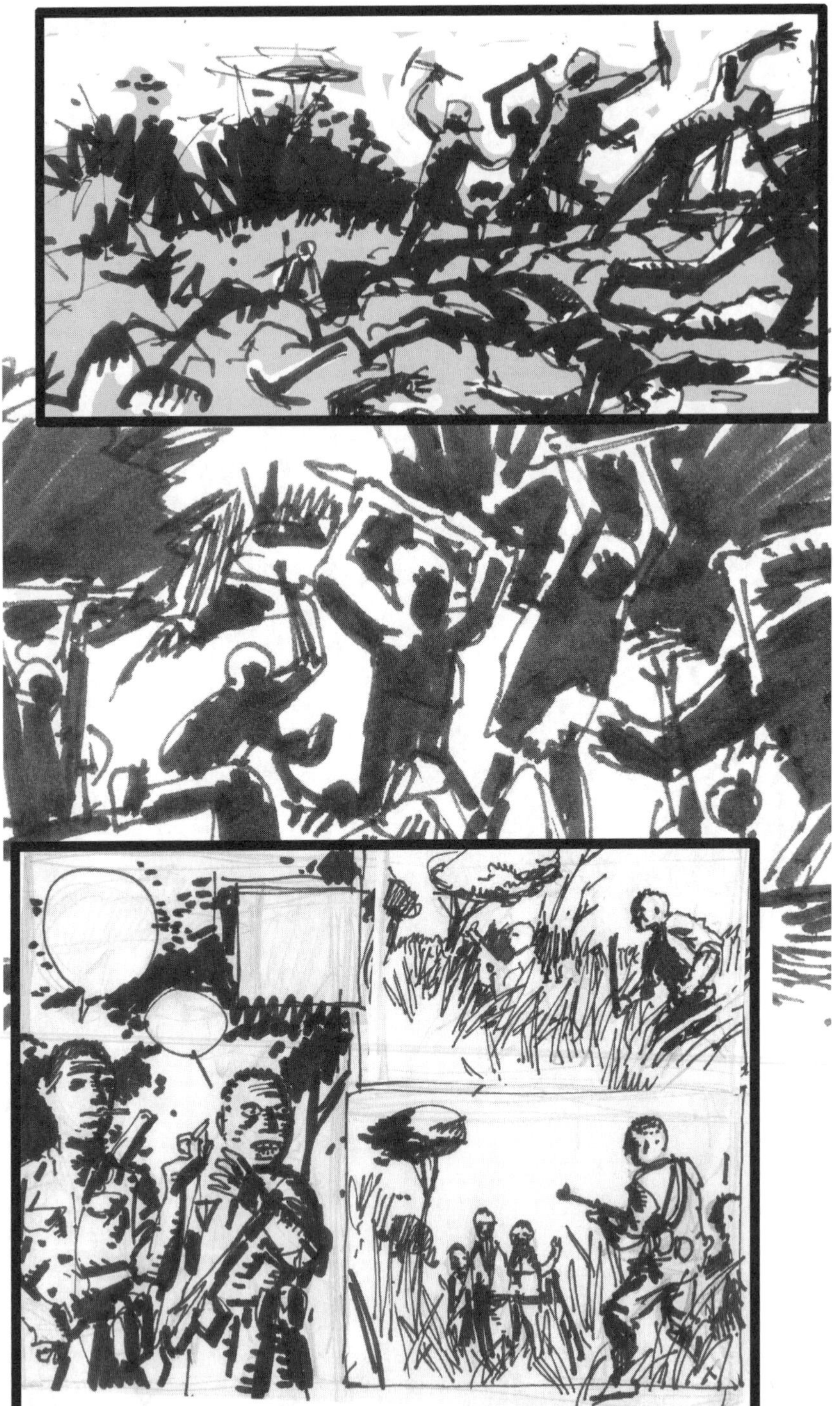

Before doing the final illustrations, Tim sketched thumbnails, small roughs of the pages including word balloons and captions, on scrap paper with marker. You can see examples of these rough drawings above. After this he drew the final art on Bristol board with a pencil and then black ink with a brush.

Notes and Sources

PROLOGUE

Two excellent recent books on the history of the Democratic Republic of Congo include Jason Stearns' *Dancing in the Glory of Monsters: The Collapse of the Congo and the Great War of Africa* (PublicAffairs, 2011) and Adam Hochschild's *King Leopold's Ghost: A Story of Greed, Terror, and Heroism in Colonial Africa* (Houghton Mifflin Harcourt, 1998).

For a more succinct summary of Congo's origins, the U.S. State Department has an excellent online primer: http://www.state.gov/r/pa/ei/bgn/2823.htm

CHAPTER ONE

The tale of schoolteacher Fidel Mboligikpele and the LRA attack on Duru in September 2008 is based mostly on the author's interviews with Mboligikpele in nearby Dungu in the fall of 2010. Additional material comes from Ferruccio Gobbi and refugees and U.N. officials in Dungu.

The broad sweeps of the narrative—time, place, and major events—are factual. I recreated dialogue based on my conversations with Mboligikpele and others; the art is based on photos I took of Mboligikpele and villages in northeastern Congo.

The LRA attacks of late 2008 have been reported in exhaustive detail by several aid groups and international agencies. The best include reports by:
U.N. High Commissioner for Refugees: http://unhcr.org/4970709d4.html
Human Rights Watch: http://www.hrw.org/sites/default/files/reports/
drc0209webwcover_1.pdf

CHAPTER TWO

The retelling of Father Ferruccio Gobbi's abduction by the LRA is based on the author's interview with Gobbi in Dungu in late 2010. In addition, Gobbi provided a written account of his experiences that included greater detail than he recalled in conversation. Visual references—scores of photos and videos—were provided by Gobbi.

Context for the Catholic Church's role in Congolese society was offered by Father Benoit Kinalegu during the author's interview with Kinalegu in Dungu.

CHAPTER THREE

The author did not meet Joseph Kony; few journalists have. This book's recounting of the early life and war career of Kony is based on the following sources:

BBC profile of Kony: http://www.bbc.co.uk/news/world-africa-17299084

International Criminal Court case against Kony and accomplices: http://www.icc-cpi.int/Menus/ICC/Situations+and+Cases/Situations/Situation+ICC+0204/Related+Cases/ICC+0204+0105/Uganda.htm

U.N. Security Council report: http://daccess-dds-ny.un.org/doc/UNDOC/GEN/N12/348/12/PDF/N1234812.pdf?OpenElement

U.S. State Department report: http://www.state.gov/p/af/rls/rm/2011/178501.htm

For more, see Peter Eichstaedt's book *First Kill Your Family: Child Soldiers of Uganda and the Lord's Resistance Army* (Chicago Review Press, 2009).

Also see Matthew Green's *The Wizard of the Nile: The Hunt for Africa's Most Wanted* (Olive Branch Press, 2008.)

CHAPTER FOUR

This brief history of the doomed Operation Lightning Thunder, a joint U.S.-African military operation aimed at encircling the LRA, is based on the author's conversations with aid workers in the DRC plus several key outside sources:

Center for Strategic and International Studies: http://csis.org/publication/lords-resistance-army

Enough Project: http://www.enoughproject.org/publications/finishing-fight-against-lra-strategy-paper

The New York Times: http://www.nytimes.com/2009/02/07/world/africa/07congo.html?pagewanted=2&_r=2&sq=uganda,%20LRA&st=cse&scp=7&

CHAPTER FIVE

The tragic tale of "Patricia" and her brother, both LRA abductees, is based on the author's interviews with both victims in Dungu in late 2010. Additional information came from Father Ernest Sugule in Dungu. The LRA characters are composites and the dialogue is recreated, but reflects extensive reporting on the LRA by multiple sources, including:

CNN: http://www.cnn.com/2011/10/23/world/africa/uganda-war-survivor/index.html

Enough Project: http://www.enoughproject.org/files/pdf/lra_survivors.pdf

U.N. High Commissioner for Refugees: http://www.unhcr.org/cgi-bin/texis/vtx/search?page=search&docid=4f88330d9&query=LRA

U.N. Office for the Coordination of Humanitarian Affairs: http://www.irinnews.org/IndepthMain.aspx?InDepthID=58&ReportID=72444

CHAPTER SIX

Sources for this sketch of Hillary Clinton's 2009 trip to the DRC and subsequent advocacy for intervention include:

The Christian Science Monitor: http://www.csmonitor.com/World/Global-News/2009/0810/clinton-in-congo-my-husband-is-not-the-secretary-of-state-i-am

The New York Times: http://www.nytimes.com/2009/08/12/world/africa/12diplo.html; and: http://www.nytimes.com/2009/08/13/world/africa/13clinton.html

U.S. State Department: http://www.state.gov/secretary/rm/2010/08/146285.htm

Visual references came from the U.S. State Department's Flickr stream: http://www.flickr.com/search/?w=9364837%40N06&q=clinton+congo&m=text

CHAPTER SEVEN

The author based the survey of peacekeeping and military advisory activities in the DRC on firsthand observation and interviews conducted in Kinshasa and eastern Congo in late 2010. The author accompanied U.S. Army troops in the capital and U.N. peacekeepers in the east. Information on the local self-defense units came from aid group Invisible Children, as seen in one of the group's videos: http://vimeo.com/22096407#at=0

The following external sources added some detail:

Allafrica.com: http://allafrica.com/stories/201110201022.html

Human Rights Watch: http://www.hrw.org/news/2009/11/02/eastern-dr-congo-surge-army-atrocities; and: http://www.hrw.org/news/2012/04/20/central-african-republic-lra-attacks-escalate

U.N.: http://www.un.org/en/peacekeeping/missions/monusco/facts.shtml

U.S. Army: http://www.army.mil/article/34756/U_S__and_DRC_in_partnership_to_train_model_Congolese_battalion/

U.S. State Department: http://2001-2009.state.gov/r/pa/prs/ps/2007/oct/94456.htm

CHAPTER EIGHT

The author based the portrait of aid group Invisible Children on interviews with group members in 2010 and 2011, plus the following external sources:

The Envoy: http://news.yahoo.com/blogs/envoy/kony2012-invisible-children-viral-video-uganda-conflict-sparks-183106657.html

Invisible Children: http://invisiblechildren.com/about/our-team/; and: http://invisiblechildren.com/critiques/

The Washington Post: http://www.washingtonpost.com/lifestyle/style/jason-russell-on-kony-his-breakdown-and-move/2012/11/15/fb70591a-2ec7-11e2-89d4-040c9330702a_story.html; and: http://www.washingtonpost.com/blogs/blogpost/post/invisible-children-founders-posing-with-guns-an-interview-with-the-photographer/2012/03/08/gIQASX68yR_blog.html

Invisible Children's famous "Kony2012" video can be seen here: http://www.youtube.com/watch?v=Y4MnpzG5Sqc

POSTSCRIPT

Source for Caesar Acellam's capture include:

AFP: http://www.google.com/hostednews/afp/article/ALeqM5gCsrEuxW0vmMtMQVtBnZqf4CqeGw?docId=CNG.2f480e256871a1acb83022961b135053.2a1

Allafrica.com: http://allafrica.com/stories/201205291020.html

The Guardian: http://www.guardian.co.uk/world/2012/may/14/uganda-forces-capture-kony-commander

The New York Times: http://www.nytimes.com/2012/05/14/world/africa/ugandan-forces-capture-rebel-army-commander.html

The Sydney Morning Herald: http://www.smh.com.au/world/end-nears-for-kony-as-top-commander-captured-20120514-1ymuk.html

Time: http://world.time.com/2012/05/14/why-the-capture-of-a-kony-lieutenant-isnt-a-big-deal/

ACKNOWLEDGMENTS

David Axe would like to thank: Matt Bors, Noah Shachtman, the staff of *Pacific Standard* magazine, Eric "Cowboy" Kapita, Benoit Kinalegu, Elisee Anidawe, Ernest Sugule, Ferruccio Gobbi, Fidel Mboligikpele, the U.N. staff and peacekeepers in Dungu, his agent, Bob Mecoy, and the editors and other staff at PublicAffairs, without whom this book would not have been possible.

Tim Hamilton would like to thank: All the other creative people at Drawbridge Studios, May Parcey, Victoria Lau, Danica Novgorodoff, Matt Bors, my agent Bob Mecoy, the fine people at PublicAffairs, and especially my supportive wife, Jean, without whom this book would not have been possible.

HOW TO HELP

THE BEST WAY TO HELP the victims of Joseph Kony and the LRA is to donate to aid groups that work directly with vulnerable Congolese communities.

The best include:

Care International: Supports more than 1,000 poverty-fighting initiatives in 84 countries including the DRC. Care International also helps Congolese victims of sexual violence. http://www.care-international.org/

Cooperazione Internazionale: An Italian organization with an office in Dungu, DRC, that focuses on assisting victims of sexual enslavement by the LRA and other armed groups. COOPI helped provide medical care and counseling to Patricia after she was freed from LRA captivity. http://coopi.org/it/home/

Invisible Children: San Diego-based Invisible Children is not an aid group, per se. Rather, it focuses on educating the public about the LRA's atrocities with its slickly-produced videos. In addition, Invisible Children oversaw the provision of early-warning radios to vulnerable towns and villages in the LRA's path. http://invisiblechildren.com/

Oxfam International: An umbrella organization for more than a dozen aid groups, Oxfam International helps provide education, health care and refugee assistance in Congo. Oxfam also produces some of the best studies of the DRC's conflicts—a vital service that guides the overall aid effort in the country. http://www.oxfam.org/en

PublicAffairs is a publishing house founded in 1997. It is a tribute to the standards, values, and flair of three persons who have served as mentors to countless reporters, writers, editors, and book people of all kinds, including me.

I. F. STONE, proprietor of *I. F. Stone's Weekly*, combined a commitment to the First Amendment with entrepreneurial zeal and reporting skill and became one of the great independent journalists in American history. At the age of eighty, Izzy published *The Trial of Socrates*, which was a national bestseller. He wrote the book after he taught himself ancient Greek.

BENJAMIN C. BRADLEE was for nearly thirty years the charismatic editorial leader of *The Washington Post*. It was Ben who gave the *Post* the range and courage to pursue such historic issues as Watergate. He supported his reporters with a tenacity that made them fearless and it is no accident that so many became authors of influential, best-selling books.

ROBERT L. BERNSTEIN, the chief executive of Random House for more than a quarter century, guided one of the nation's premier publishing houses. Bob was personally responsible for many books of political dissent and argument that challenged tyranny around the globe. He is also the founder and longtime chair of Human Rights Watch, one of the most respected human rights organizations in the world.

·   ·   ·

For fifty years, the banner of Public Affairs Press was carried by its owner Morris B. Schnapper, who published Gandhi, Nasser, Toynbee, Truman, and about 1,500 other authors. In 1983, Schnapper was described by *The Washington Post* as "a redoubtable gadfly." His legacy will endure in the books to come.

Peter Osnos, *Founder and Editor-at-Large*